PRAISE FOR
THE TWENTYSOMETHING
HANDBOOK

"Nora Bradbury-Haehl has written a gamechanger. Her latest book provides everything a twentysomething person needs to know (and probably doesn't) to lead a productive, meaningful, and self-sufficient life. Whether the topic is relationships, housing, self-care, finances, or the job market, *The Twentysomething Handbook* offers practical, actionable tips. But even more important, this guide helps young adults do what they need and hope for most: making their lives matter. Highly recommended!"

> **—Dr. Michele Borba, educational psychologist**
> **and author of *Thrivers: The Surprising Reasons***
> ***Why Some Kids Struggle While Others Shine***

"What a terrific resource, and not just for young adults! *The Twentysomething Handbook* is a guidebook for navigating a chaotic and life-giving stage in your journey. Though focused on young adults and the myriad issues they confront, this handbook is valuable for anyone experiencing life's transitions. Not only does Nora clearly describe a wide range of lifestyle concerns including money, jobs, relationships, renting, and even meals, she explores the personal challenges of dealing with transitions, grief, forgiveness, mental health, and more. The voices, insights, and experiences of young adults are interspersed throughout the book, adding realism and authenticity to the insights provided. Each chapter also includes action items and nuggets of advice that succinctly capture the focus. *The Twentysomething Handbook* is a comprehensive companion for everyone meandering through these wonderful years."

> **—Robert J. McCarty, DMin, pastoral ministry**
> **and leadership consultant and author of**
> ***Faith Talk* and *Going, Going, Gone***

"Nora Bradbury-Haehl has penned a treasure-trove of discernment, real-world practical advice, and self-help methods. Twentysomethings will find this book indispensable because of its down-to-earth candor from their peers and those who have mentored them."

—Mike Hayes, director of young adult ministry in the Diocese of Cleveland, founder of BustedHalo.com, and author of *Loving Work* and *Googling God*

"In my years of working in campus ministry, it has become increasingly clear that young adults struggle with transitions, and that we have very few tools and structures to help manage those complicated transitions. In her first book, *The Freshman Survival Guide*, Nora Bradbury-Haehl brought a wealth of wisdom and experience to the transition from home to campus. In her new book she's tackled the next critical inflection point: from campus to establishing one's own independent (and interdependent) life. For young adults wondering, "I'm twenty-five, why don't I know how to cook, manage my finance, or make friends?" this book is brimming with good advice, real wisdom, and reassurance. If the expectations and requirements of 'adulting' seem daunting or anxiety-producing, this book isn't just helpful, it's a lifeline."

—Father Larry Rice, CSP, former director at University Catholic Center, Austin

"*The Twentysomething Handbook* is a jam-packed comprehensive guide that gives twentysomethings the essential information they need to make a smooth transition to everything after college!

—Harlan Cohen, *New York Times* bestselling author of *The Naked Roommate* and *Win or Learn*

THE
TWENTYSOMETHING
HANDBOOK

ALSO BY NORA BRADBURY-HAEHL

The Freshman Survival Guide

THE
TWENTYSOMETHING
HANDBOOK

Everything You **Actually** Need to Know About **Real Life**

NORA BRADBURY-HAEHL

Bestselling Author of *The Freshman Survival Guide*

NELSON
BOOKS

An Imprint of Thomas Nelson

The Twentysomething Handbook

© 2021 by Nora Bradbury-Haehl

Published in Nashville, Tennessee, by Nelson Books, an imprint of Thomas Nelson. Nelson Books and Thomas Nelson are registered trademarks of HarperCollins Christian Publishing, Inc.

The author is represented by Joelle Delbourgo Associates, Inc., 101 Park Street, Montclair, NJ 07042.

Thomas Nelson titles may be purchased in bulk for educational, business, fundraising, or sales promotional use. For information, please e-mail SpecialMarkets@ThomasNelson.com.

Any internet addresses, phone numbers, or company or product information printed in this book are offered as a resource and are not intended in any way to be or to imply an endorsement by Thomas Nelson, nor does Thomas Nelson vouch for the existence, content, or services of these sites, phone numbers, companies, or products beyond the life of this book.

Library of Congress Cataloging-in-Publication Data

Names: Bradbury-Haehl, Nora, author.
Title: The twentysomething handbook : everything you actually need to know about real life / Nora Bradbury-Haehl.
Description: Nashville : Thomas Nelson, 2021. | Includes bibliographical references. | Summary: "The ultimate, one-stop-shop resource for navigating and winning at life's most bewildering period"-- Provided by publisher.
Identifiers: LCCN 2020042110 (print) | LCCN 2020042111 (ebook) | ISBN 9781400222544 (paperback) | ISBN 9781400222551 (epub)
Subjects: LCSH: Youth--Social aspects. | Youth--Economic aspects. | Life skills.
Classification: LCC HQ796 .B686124 2021 (print) | LCC HQ796 (ebook) | DDC 646.700835--dc23
LC record available at https://lccn.loc.gov/2020042110
LC ebook record available at https://lccn.loc.gov/2020042111

Printed in the United States of America

21 22 23 24 25 LSC 10 9 8 7 6 5 4 3 2 1

To Greg, for knowing I could do it and
being with me while I did.

CONTENTS

Introduction   XIII

PART 1: BUILDING A LIFE YOU LOVE

Chapter 1:   Where's Home? Turning Your Current
             City into Your New Hometown   3
Chapter 2:   Fantastic Jobs and Where to Find
             Them (And How to Keep Them)   17
Chapter 3:   My Place: Apartment Hunting and
             Apartment Dwelling   37
Chapter 4:   Adulting at Your Parents' House   57

PART 2: THE BASICS OF TWENTYSOMETHING LIFE

Chapter 5:   Shared Spaces vs. Solitary Places:
             Roommates, House Rules, and
             Cleaning Routines   71

CONTENTS

Chapter 6:   Mmmmm, Delish! (But Also Affordable,
              Attainable, and Healthy-ish)   93
Chapter 7:   My Stuff, My Self: Sorting Out
              Essentials from Excess   109
Chapter 8:   Budgeting for Beginners: Making
              the Most of Your Money   119

PART 3: REAL RELATIONSHIPS FOR REAL LIFE

Chapter 9:   Not a Kid Anymore: Navigating
              Family Relationships as an Adult   147
Chapter 10:   Fast Friends: The Work and Reward
              of Creating Your Circle   161
Chapter 11:   You're Amazing! How to Find
              Someone Else Who Thinks So Too   185

PART 4: SELF-CARE SYMPOSIUM

Chapter 12:   The Good News About Your
              Bad Habits   201
Chapter 13:   How's Your Brain Doing? Mental
              Health for Twentysomethings   211
Chapter 14:   Grieving at Twentysomething: Dealing
              with Death and Other Big Losses   229

PART 5: BECOMING YOURSELF

Chapter 15:   Getting a Second Chance:
              Forgiveness Is for Grown-Ups
              (This Means You)   247

Chapter 16: The Power of Difference: Why
Diversity and Inclusion Matter   261
Chapter 17: Making Your Life Matter   273

Find Yourself A . . .   281
Renter's Glossary   285
Acknowledgments   293
Notes   297
About the Author   303

INTRODUCTION

Dear Twentysomething,

Hi, I'm Nora. For more than twenty-five years I've worked with teens and twentysomethings in churches, camps, and leadership programs. I've been really (*really*) lucky to spend my career in the world of late nights and laughing till you cry and singing loudly and letting your guard down. The world of discovering who you are and realizing that there actually are people who understand what it's like to be you. I've spent my life in the kinds of places that form deep bonds; the kinds of bonds where people, when they're having trouble in life, come back to check in. Sometimes it's been a few months since we've talked, sometimes it's been a few years. Sometimes they're touching base to ask for advice or support. Often, it's because they need to be reminded of who they were because they're working really hard to become who they want to be.

That's where this book comes from. It comes from being a part of people's lives and wanting the best for them. I want the best for you too. It's probably a little weird for me to tell you that (since we've only just met), but I'm doing it anyway. I do want the best for you, and I hope this book helps you get there.

At first glance it might seem like this book is about the easy, straightforward things that everyone ought to know: how to find an apartment or cook a meal or make a budget. And it is. (Though you may have already discovered that many of the things that are supposed to be easy, are not easy at all.) Here in these pages you can find help for all the tasks and to-dos of twentysomething life; things that maybe you should have learned by now but somehow missed. But there's more than that.

One of the twentysomething voices you'll hear throughout the book, Emily, put it really well:

I think it's worth acknowledging that this is a time when the game has changed, and that it's okay to feel out of sorts or like things are just hard(er). That it can be an amazing time full of growth and figuring things out and starting to curate habits for the rest of your life, but if you're not experiencing all the wonderful upsides of that growth, you're not somehow missing out on the biggest and best time of your life. There are new challenges in each season of life, and this feeling that everything is tough and you haven't quite arrived yet—that things are not as bright and shiny as you thought they would be when you graduated high school a few years ago—passes. Those (lousy) jobs and the just-for-now relationships and the fish-out-of-water gasp of a new town, the dive bars and the roommates and calling a "real" adult each time something breaks—they're not forever. One day you look back and realize you've figured it out. And this book is here to help you along the way, from a place of respect for how much work it takes to walk into your twenties and emerge out the other side into adulthood.

As you go through the book, you'll find features that can help focus on the topic at hand, explain it further, or invite you to start taking action in that area of your life:

TWENTYSOMETHING TIP: Each chapter opens with a quick idea that will give you a feel for what it's about. The tip can serve as a jumping-off point for your own thoughts and discussions about the chapter ahead.

TWENTYSOMETHING TALK: These are from real people—like Emily—telling it like it is, or like it was for them. I gathered input from people across the country through surveys and social media. They share their stories and struggles throughout the book.

NOW DO THIS: These are small ways to start taking action. Use these steps to get started and move from thinking about what could be, to making it happen.

YOU ACTUALLY NEED TO KNOW: If I could leave you with one thought, here it is. Each chapter ends with a nugget of advice small enough to put in your pocket, literally and metaphorically, and carry out into the world with you.

The content of the book is the stuff that twentysomethings have been talking about with me for years. Things like growing into the person that you want to be, managing relationships well, pursuing diversity, and questions about the harder parts of life. What about grief? Mental health? Addiction? Questions like, "How can I continue to be a part of the family I grew up in when the person I've become just doesn't fit there anymore?" And, "I want my life to matter; how can I make that happen?" It takes courage to even consider a lot of these questions. It's sometimes easier to just keep chugging along and hope they resolve themselves. That brings me to my final point.

Many of the twentysomethings I talk to feel like they are the only one. The only one who doesn't know, who doesn't have it handled, who hates their job, who can't figure out relationships, who is happy then miserable then happy again. Maybe the most important thing this book is about is remembering that you're not alone in the weirdness that is being a twentysomething.

One of my hopes—even before I began writing—was that this book would be a way for twentysomethings to connect with one another. If you want to go deeper, do better with a group, or hear what other people think—come visit us at www.twentysomethinghandbook.com for ideas on how to use *The Twentysomething Handbook* and connect to a broader community. You'll find discussion guides and instructions on how to start or join a Twentysomething Circle in your city or online. If you are a librarian, community leader, religious leader, HR professional, or anyone else who wants to know more about using this book to help the twentysomethings in your community or organization, there are resources at the website for you too.

Let's figure this out together,
Nora

PART 1

BUILDING A LIFE YOU LOVE

CHAPTER 1

WHERE'S HOME?

Turning Your Current City into Your New Hometown

TWENTYSOMETHING TIP: Learning to love where you are, even if it's not right where you want to be, can make life less of a struggle and more of an adventure. It's okay to miss the place that used to be home while you work to make this new place your home too.

Does your new city feel like home yet? When you stop and think about it, it would be surprising if it did. You spent time, had experiences, and built relationships in the places you lived before. You made memories with people you cared about and who cared about you. You did some significant growing in those places, and you may have nostalgia for the times gone by: the places you used to go to celebrate special occasions, the things you used to do for fun. Once you're gone from a place you can even miss the things that used to drive you crazy about it. You can miss the weather, the crush and bustle of a city street, the quiet isolation of wide-open fields, or whatever was particular to the place you called home.

Often the place wasn't as important as the people you were sharing it with. Those associations of joy and calm, of friendship or family, can make our previous place seem like a better or easier place to live. In contrast, a new, unfamiliar place doesn't seem to stand a chance of living up to all that. Maybe the place where you're from doesn't hold a lot of positive memories for you, and you're just glad to be out of there. But it was familiar and predictable, and there's something to be said for that. Either way, it took time for the place that was home to be home for you. It won't happen overnight, but with a little effort and a spirit of exploration, you may be surprised to find how much affection you can develop for a place that's new to you.

Prep

There's plenty you can do before you get to your new city to ease the feeling that everything's hitting you at once. Visit the city website and see what resources and information are available. If you're headed to a big city, get your hands on a guidebook for tourists. They usually include information on neighborhoods and nightlife along with sights to see. Change your address by going to www.usps.com and filling out the form to have your mail forwarded. Update your new address for any subscriptions you have as well.

Does your current bank have branches in your new city? If not, look into opening an account with a new bank that does. If you have a vehicle and you'll be moving out of state, visit the DMV website for your new city. Check on each of the following: requirements and fees to register your vehicle, whether you'll need to get a license in your new state or can just transfer your old one, and how much time you have to do it. Some states allow you to do all of this online, others require an in-person vision test or exam.

Time frames and fees vary from state to state, so it's worth looking into it ahead of time. While you're on the DMV website, check to see if you can register to vote online. Once you have moving dates you can set up getting your utilities turned on in your new place so you'll have lights, heat, and internet when you arrive. Fill all your prescriptions before your move, and if you can get a few months in advance, do it.

The Basics

One of the first things you'll encounter in a new place is the challenge of meeting basic, immediate needs. Assuming you already have a roof overhead, where do you get groceries? If you're driving, where do you get gas for your car? If you're taking public transportation, what's the best train or bus to take, and how long will your commute be? If you have pets, where do you get their food or walk them? Where's the nearest vet? What about a doctor for you? A therapist? Are there support groups or recovery meetings nearby? Where will you get a haircut or buy a nail to hang a picture? Where's the post office, the bank, the DMV, city hall?

There's a lot to think about when you move to a new place, which can be overwhelming. But don't panic. You'll discover answers to many of these questions as you go along. When you need a whatever-it-is, you'll take the time to look for a solution then. If you're someone who likes to be prepared, though, check out the "Find Yourself A . . ." list at the back of this book (or make a list of your own) and start looking around for the people, places, and services you may need in your new place. Highlight the ones you may need early on and prioritize finding them.

Settle In

Now find the bagel shop, the pizza place, the mom-and-pop diner, the nearest place with live music, and a coffee shop that's not a national chain. Get your library card and register to vote. Follow local news and social media to plug into what's going on around you and get the local vibe. Local journalists' social media pages will often give you a close-up look at neighborhood and regional events you might otherwise miss out on. Get an insider's view of your new town by wandering off the beaten path. Visit the farmers' markets. As you really start to get to know your new home, get off the highway and take the side routes and old roads that were there before the interstates. You may see a whole different aspect of the city.

TWENTYSOMETHING TALK

To make a new city feel like home, I started with thinking of my favorite things and places back home and tried to find a few stand-ins for when I was homesick. Not replacements. Stand-ins. I found my new local favorite pizza place. I found the library. I joined the gym. I started a routine. But I think it's even more important to find what makes your new place unique and gives you reasons to embrace it. I found a new hobby that didn't really work at home but fit perfectly in my new life. And, of course, finding new friends made all the difference. —Abby

Explore

Once you've got your immediate concerns under control, take a look around. Make exploring your new city into a hobby. There are several different ways to go about it. An easy place to start is shopping. You could probably order a lot of what you'll need online, and for the sake of convenience, sometimes you may need to do that. But there are benefits to hitting the street to find what you're looking for in your new neighborhood. As you look for what you need, you'll come across people and places you didn't expect. If your neighborhood is walkable, all the better. You'll see things you'd miss otherwise. You won't always have time to explore, but when you do, don't be afraid to burn a little free time discovering what's nearby.

Another approach is to turn yourself into a tour guide for friends and family that may visit. Preparing for visitors is also a good way to fight homesickness. Find out what places everyone should see when they come to your new town. Visit those places now or at least learn more about them—how to get to them and how much they cost. What are the local sports teams, big and small, especially the ones you can afford to go see? Are there any scenic spots or natural wonders? What about renowned places to eat or bands, theater groups, or musical ensembles to see? What museums should you visit or which college campuses might people want to see?

Take a historical and anthropological approach to your exploration. Find out who lived here first. What indigenous people called this place home? What was their story, are they still present, and what place names, foods, or cultural influences are still evident because of them? Were they displaced, by whom, when and how? What immigrant groups have lived here? When did those waves of people come, and what were their stories?

Who lives here now, and where did they come from? What are poverty rates like, what areas are gentrified, and where did the people who used to live there go? Have there been any famous folks from any of those groups? Who are the local heroes? Are there statues or parks, highways or stadiums, named for them?

If you're more of a science nerd than a history nerd, try taking a geological and environmental approach to your new town. How was this landscape formed and when? What are its unique features? How has it impacted the development and use of natural resources? How are those resources used or overused now? Are there wetlands or waterways or aquifers to learn more about? What about unique or protected species? Find out about hiking and biking trails, kayaking spots, or other ways to explore waterways and nature.

There are many other ways to discover what's unique or wonderful about the place that's becoming home. Check out activist groups, art, architecture, the chamber of commerce, churches and houses of worship, festivals, parades. Get involved with politics, philanthropy, service/volunteering. The list is endless.

TWENTYSOMETHING TALK

Not knowing anyone in a new city is the *worst*. I get really into nesting whenever I move somewhere scary and new—I make my home a cozy, happy place that I'm excited to return to at the end of the day. Even if it takes a while to build friends who I want to go out with, at least I can feel happy in my home. —Lilly

The few times I have moved, I started with work. Making work feel like home can help you make new friends. Many times this has branched off into other friendships. Work is a good place to start. I also suggest finding any space that can make you feel at home and a space that you can call your own. —Tyler

Weather and Other Natural Dangers

Are you moving from a warm place to a colder place? Or a dry place to a humid place? You might be from a place where the weather was pretty even, and now you're living someplace with extremes. It can take a little time to adjust. If you've never lived in a place with extreme temperatures—either cold or hot—getting the safety parts of that down is important. In some instances, it can be life-or-death important.

If you're moving someplace that experiences seriously cold weather for the first time, proper gear is vital. Even if you're not an outdoorsy person, you will enjoy greater safety and greater comfort with a good coat (not just a cute one), extra gloves, real hats (wool, not acrylic), and insulated boots. If you have a car, learn how to prep it for winter with things like snow tires and fluid changes, and put together a little safety box to keep in the trunk in case you get stranded or stuck in a snow bank. Learn about frostbite and hypothermia and how to prevent them. Pay attention to local media for windchill warnings, lake-effect snows, and blizzard warnings.

If you're coming from a place with moderate to cold weather

and going to a place with heat, consider these two words: cotton sheets. Actually, you're going to want to reassess most of your fabric choices. Some for comfort, some for safety. Lightweight and lighter-colored cottons are better in the heat. You might be surprised to find that locals favor long sleeves and hats. Wear sunscreen on your face (at least), if you'll be outside for any length of time. Get in the habit of carrying water with you. If you're in dry heat for the first time, watch out for dehydration.

TWENTYSOMETHING TALK

Sweat spots are so real, especially in high humidity (think Florida, summers in the South). When you get dressed, examine the color/material/fit of your top. How likely is it to show sweat on your back or under your arms? If you have to be outside (like for a commute), carry deodorant with you. You're gonna sweat. It's gonna be gross. During the summer in a place like DC, lots of walking or biking commuters wear workout clothes and change when they get where they're going. —Emily

If you're driving, park in the shade if you can. A few things to keep in your car: a windshield sunshade, a towel to cover the seat, and clean jugs of water in the trunk (especially in arid heat). Water solves a lot of problems and can help in several kinds of emergencies. No water causes problems. Know that you'll be swapping your heating bill for a cooling bill and keep an eye on that bill. Compare it with local averages. If there's something wrong with your AC unit, it will show up there. A bedroom fan can help keep costs down. Make sure you check with locals or keep watch on local media for concerns over amoebas, which inhabit still, warm fresh water. There are places you just don't swim when it gets hot enough in the summer.

In any new environment, get familiar with biological dangers. If there are poisonous plants, venomous insects or snakes, disease-carrying wildlife, find out what they look like and what to do if you encounter them. If relevant to your area, take time to learn how to be prepared for the following: earthquakes, floods, extreme storms, tornadoes, hurricanes, wildfires, and smog warnings (which are a combination of naturally caused and human caused). Even if they don't happen often, you'll know what to do if the need arises.

Cultural Differences

If you've always lived in an urban area, you may not realize that gas stations aren't on every corner in a more rural setting, and grocery stores and restaurants aren't always open late. If you've never lived in an urban area, getting used to the extra safety precautions (lock everything, every time) and learning to deal with other challenges of urban life, things like panhandlers or aggressive drivers, can take a little time. The pace of life and conversation can be different between North and South, East and West. "How are you doing today?" in one region is a necessary courtesy before any business begins; in another place it could be considered nosy or intrusive. In some places religion is politely avoided and in others folks wear it on their sleeves.

If you belong to any kind of minority group, moving from a less diverse place to a more diverse one can be a huge relief. You may, for the first time in your life, just blend into the crowd. The other way round, moving to a less diverse or less progressive place, you may suddenly find yourself very much in the minority and the object of people's curiosity or prejudices. The curiosity part (possibly sweet, possibly annoying) might not be too bad, and you can decide how much you want to play the ambassador and how much you want to point people in other directions to educate themselves. If you belong to a targeted group—racial, religious, cultural—be aware and be prudent. Finding yourself in a place where you are under attack or suspicion because of who you are or how you look can be a rude and dangerous awakening. Find out how other minorities fare in your new city and what they do to stay safe. Has there been violence? Are there organized groups targeting minorities? Has the role of law enforcement been positive or negative? Look for groups that are organizing for the protection and defense of minorities. They can be a resource for prevention and advocacy.

TWENTYSOMETHING TALK

When I moved to New York City right after college, I ended up feeling *so* depressed. Part of it was loneliness (fueled by little money, which makes it hard to hang out in the city). Part of it was not having a solid network of people to hang out with and lean on. Part of it was a lack of nature (I hadn't realized how important that was to me), and there were a million other factors. It took some time to figure out those life-style things that made a positive difference in my daily life—eating a balanced diet, getting regular exercise, getting sunshine and nature time, having a home that felt like I could invite people in. —Eric

---

NOW DO THIS: Choose one idea or activity from this chap-ter. Do it and write down what you found out about your city.

YOU ACTUALLY NEED TO KNOW: Even if where you're liv-ing is your dream destination, you may still experience hiccups as you get used to life in a new town. Get acquainted with your city and surrounding area and get thinking about how to make the most of the experience.

CHAPTER 2

FANTASTIC JOBS AND WHERE TO FIND THEM

(And How to Keep Them)

TWENTYSOMETHING TIP: Learning to navigate the professional world of applications and interviews takes time. That's followed by learning your way around the world of bosses, coworkers, and the daily grind of work. Help can come from surprising places that you might already have access to.

How's your work life going? Has it not even started yet? Are you already sick of it? Are you passing time in a just-for-the-money job while, in your spare time, you continue to pursue the career you really want? Welcome to your twenties. In one Harris survey almost 80 percent of workers in their twenties said they wanted to change careers.[1] Another survey identified "finding a job that they're passionate about" as the top concern for people between the ages of twenty-five and thirty-three.[2] For many Gen Z workers, who watched their parents struggle through the Great Recession, job security and salary are important. In spite of that, working for an organization that matches their values is a priority.[3]

If you've never worked in a professional environment before, the demands of the work world can take some adjusting to. At a new job you're getting used to the range of personalities and the pace of work while figuring out how to meet other people's expectations. Different companies and organizations have a wide range of strengths and shortcomings. Some of these are worth adapting to, some need to be challenged, and others are better to walk away from. Become an observer and learner but remember to hang on to the values that matter most.

Job Hunting

The job search can be pretty daunting if you're just getting started. Where do you even begin? A good first step, before you send anything out to anyone, is to check your online reputation. Hiring managers will most likely do a quick search. So now is the time to do some cleanup work on your social media accounts. Search your name, check what images come up, and be sure your privacy settings are strong across all your social media accounts. You don't have to erase yourself, but check that what is publicly out there about you puts forward the person you want to present as a job candidate.

Next, is your resume in top-notch shape? If not, or if you're not feeling confident about it, look at the resumes of other people in your industry. Take note of what format seems to be preferred. Ask friends or connections in your field if they would look it over for you before you start sending it out. Your college's placement office or career center, even if your degree isn't complete yet, is there for your benefit. The counselors working there can often help you in your job search in many different ways, and they're sure to have an overabundance of resources when it comes to resume writing.

Simpler is almost always better for resumes. Be specific but brief. Unless your industry calls for it, avoid long descriptions about what you've done in previous jobs or in your research. Instead, use quick bullet points, knowing that you'll have the opportunity to answer detailed questions in your interview. Your cover letter is the place to point out anything you want to highlight on your resume and can give your interviewer the hint to ask more about it.

Put your networks to work. The people you are already connected to may well know someone you want to get connected to or someone who would be helpful for you to talk with. Let friends and family know you're looking—even if the link is a distant one, nearly any contact you have is worth tapping into. Most people remember what it feels like to be looking and are happy to help you. If they aren't in a position to help, you're none the worse for asking. When there's a big pile of resumes on someone's desk or in their inbox, that personal connection can get yours pulled out of the pile.

TWENTYSOMETHING TALK

I hate networking, but I have to admit that it's been a godsend for me. Take advantage of your friends' and family's contacts. You have nothing to lose by cold-emailing people, name-dropping whoever it is gave you their contact info, and asking for an informational interview. Keep your resume updated. Always look professional for interviews, even if the job won't require it. Don't be afraid to apply for something you're not quite qualified for. Maybe the company is willing to provide extra training if they can find the right fit for them. The worst they can tell you is no and then you're back in the same place you were by not applying at all. —Brandon

---

Do You Have Any Questions?

At the end of many job interviews, the interviewer will ask, "Do you have any questions for me?" Instead of looking like a deer in the headlights, it's always a good idea to have a few questions prepared. (And it's okay to have them written on an index card if you're afraid you'll forget.) It's one more chance to show the company you're thoughtful and prepared, and it's your chance to get some of the information you may need if you're deciding between a few different job offers. Ask about things you're genuinely interested in and you'll come across as sincere and prepared. You can ask questions about: accountability, supervision, training and orientation, who is on the team, what the performance review system is like, what the challenges of the role are, how it fits into the larger organization, and what the upsides (besides a paycheck) are of working at the company.

Handling Rejection and Disappointment

Whatever you do, do not take it personally if you don't get the interview, don't get called back, or don't get the job. There is almost no way for you to know what the company's internal operations and priorities are. You cannot tell whether the folks you're up against have an inside connection. You won't know if the budget for the position dried up, the company is reorganizing, or they decided to wait until next quarter to bring a new hire on. It is maddening to be on the waiting end of things, but try not to get discouraged. If you're finding you're not getting calls or you're struggling in the interviews you do get, revisit some of the earlier steps. Remember you can do everything perfectly, make no mistakes, and still not get the job.

What Matters Most

You may be working at a job that you know is not your dream job, but, for whatever reason (debt, the need for income for your family), your dreams are on hold. Or maybe you're still figuring out what your dream job actually is. You've probably been involved in at least one exercise somewhere along your educational journey to help you figure out what you're good at and what a good career path might be for you. Dr. Christine Whelan is a clinical professor in the School of Human Ecology at the University of Wisconsin-Madison and the author of *The Big Picture: A Guide to Finding Your Purpose in Life*. In the college courses she teaches she helps people address the big questions like: Who am I? What is my passion and purpose? Where do I belong? She suggests, rather than submitting to the pressure of having our careers define us, that we try to have a purpose mindset about all the parts of our lives:

> The first question most people ask is, "What do you do?" And while it is certainly ideal to have your purpose aligned with your career goals, it's not worth being unemployed if you can't make it happen. In a survey I conducted in 2016, only 36 percent of people between the ages of eighteen and twenty-four said that the career path they had chosen was aligned with their life purpose. However, as they head into the job market, 69 percent of young adults say they would be willing to take a cut in pay to work at a job that allowed them to focus on more meaningful work.[4]

As you begin to figure out what matters most to you and why, start thinking about ways to find meaning and purpose beyond your work life. If you're able to have some (or even all) of your work life be a part of that, great. If not, know that purpose is something you can pursue in different ways at different times in your life.

Getting Started at Your New Job

In a multigenerational workplace a younger person is often at risk of being treated as a kid rather than a colleague. You may find, working alongside people your parents' ages, that you also feel like a kid. One way to combat that is to defy the stereotypes. To be taken seriously, take things seriously.

1. Be prepared to fill out new hire paperwork. This process is fairly standard across industries. You'll need your identification, a bank account, a blank voided check or bank letter for direct deposit, and your social security number. This is your first impression with your coworkers. Not having these things can come across as immature.

2. Be scrupulous with your phone use at work. Depending on the generations you're working with, what is normal for you (looking something up on your phone while in a meeting, checking your calendar, replying to a text message) can come across as rude or inattentive—even

if what you're tending to is work related. It's not fair. But you'll benefit from understanding how others might perceive your behavior. Different generations have different relationships with their devices. Be aware of those differences.

3. Be a courteous coworker. Clean up after yourself. Don't leave trash or dirty dishes around. In an open office, be aware of how music, loud phone calls, and smells (food, scented products) can impact others, and be as considerate as you can. Don't swear and don't say sexist or racist things, even if others do.

4. Don't get sucked into gossip or office politics. Disengage without coming across as judgmental or unsupportive.

5. Understand that your work phone and your work computer, if issued by your workplace, are not private. Most workplaces have written policies that allow them access to anything on devices that belong to them. Often, they do not look unless there is a problem, but if they find anything inappropriate, it can be grounds for a reprimand or dismissal.

6. Ask questions. Be sure you understand what is being asked of you and how things are done at this particular workplace. Don't be afraid to follow up a meeting with a quick email confirming, "Here's what I understood we decided on. Is that right?" Doing so is a great tool to keep track of what you're responsible for and a good defense if someone else on your team is less responsible.

7. If you make a mistake, own up to it as soon as you can. Don't wait for someone else to discover it. Everyone makes mistakes; the good employees are the ones who notice their mistakes quickly and let the right people know how they plan to make amends.

Being new on the job is always a challenge. It can be even more complex if your workplace doesn't have a strong orientation or training program for new hires. If you're lucky enough to have someone showing you the ropes, make the most of it. Pay close attention, ask questions about anything you don't understand, and don't be afraid to take notes. If there's a lot to learn, you'll be glad you wrote some of it down. Some things will be covered in your employee handbook, organizational charts, and other written materials that you can refer to. Some companies are great at recording their standard operating procedures, and others are shockingly bad at it. If you're not finding the information you need, ask! Being new is the perfect time to ask lots of questions and clarify how things are done in this particular workplace. It's okay, especially at the beginning, to admit that you may have missed a step in your training or to double-check that you're doing things the right way.

Finding a Mentor

A mentor is an experienced person often in the same field (or a similar one) as you. A mentor can answer questions, help you set goals, give you feedback on projects, and help you grow in your career. Mentorship can happen within the structure of a formal program. If you've never had a mentor before and you have the opportunity to, opt for connecting with one through a program. It can be a great place to experience the benefits, learn the boundaries, and find out how to make the most of a mentoring relationship. Some workplaces provide mentoring programs, as do many networking organizations.

A mentoring relationship can also be informal. An informal mentorship might be the organic result of a preexisting relationship or can result from a new connection. Mentors can be especially helpful for those belonging to groups facing discrimination at higher rates: women, people of color, and people with disabilities. You can often find formal or informal opportunities for mentorship through the same organizations that you connect to for other kinds of workplace support and training.

If you're having a hard time finding a mentor, look at your network, where you're working now, places you've interned, people you know through friends and family, people involved in your hobbies. Even if you don't find an in-person mentor, you can adopt someone you respect and admire (or a few someones) as your virtual mentor. Identify people in your industry whose accomplishments inspire you and whose trajectory you'd like to emulate. Follow them on social media and interact there. Join their groups. Read their books. Learn the stories of their success and let them be your teachers and coaches.

Dealing with Difficult
People at Work

We've all encountered people who are hard to get along with—teachers or coaches, classmates or teammates. Interacting with them is never easy, and even the most cheerful among us can get worn out and fed up. When a coworker or a supervisor has a difficult personality, things can get very complicated. You're often dealing with that person on a regular basis, and even if the negative nonsense doesn't happen every time, after a few negative interactions you may begin dreading work and feel as though you're just waiting for the next bad thing to happen. Fortunately there are several steps you can take if you find yourself stuck with a crab, a bully, a gossip, or a harasser.

The Crab

This coworker comes to work in a bad mood, then takes it out on whoever is unfortunate enough to cross their path. The most important thing to remember is to not take the Crab personally. You can't make this person happy. Or, if you can, it is rarely in a lasting way. Especially if you tend to be a people pleaser, put your protective coating on before you interact with the Crab. Gently observing aloud that they seem to be having a hard day can sometimes get you enough of a break in the crankiness to get what you need from the Crab. And if the Crab is unappreciated at work and you can show some appreciation, you might be able to turn things around.

The Bully

This coworker may have the boss's ear or pretend to have authority because the Bully feels good when they have power. That might take the form of pushing their work off on other people, taking credit for other people's success, or being overly competitive or aggressive. Make peace if you can. Bullies can be placated if you can play along with their need to have their ego fed. The day may come where you have to stand up and call them on their nonsense though. Most will crumble when someone finally (metaphorically) pushes back, but try to be sure a few other coworkers have your back.

The Gossip

This colleague seems to have the inside scoop on everyone's personal lives and all office conflict. It's often their own insecurity talking, but be cautious with the Gossip. If they're talking to you about everyone else, odds are they are talking to everyone else about you. Be polite, but don't get too cozy. The Gossip is rarely loyal to anyone but themselves.

The Harasser

Whether coworker or supervisor, the Harasser will usually start by floating a few test balloons to check your boundaries: an inappropriate joke, a little bit of intimidation (the Harasser has a bit of the Bully in them), or even straight-up sexual advances. Often the Harasser has pull in the organization and will target someone new or lower in the ranks than they are. Sometimes this behavior is so shocking that you might react by laughing awkwardly at a joke or freezing. If you encounter the Harasser, tell someone you trust and document the incident by writing down what happened and the date and time. If you decide to act, having a record of what happened and when will be important. Reporting harassment is a calculated risk. Human resources can be helpful, but keep in mind they work for your company and are there to protect your employer.

. . . .

Understanding the line between a cranky boss who needs to be handled carefully and someone who is harassing you or discriminating against you is important. Federal laws protect US workers against discrimination based on race, religion, gender, orientation, age, disabilities, and pregnancy. All workers are also federally protected against harassment, be it sexual, verbal, physical, or cyber harassment. The Equal Employment Opportunity Commission (EEOC) has more information on harassment and how to take action against it at www.eeoc.gov/harassment.

Dealing with difficult people is part of life, and someone who is a challenge for you to deal with at the beginning of a job may grow on you over time as you learn how to get along. If problems continue, though, don't resign yourself to being miserable at work. There are steps you can take to change your situation. If your supervisor is someone you trust, see if you can be assigned to teams that don't include the difficult person or ask if work can be divided differently to minimize contact with that person.

Work Friends: The Pros and Cons

Workplace friendships are great. Making friends at work, especially if you're in a new city, can take the edge off that initial loneliness. It can give you a whole network of connections beyond work as you meet the friends of your work friends and begin to build your own web. Work friends also make work easier. You'll look forward to seeing the familiar faces of those people who help you push through hard days and who you can count on to help out with a tight deadline or difficult project. But take friendships slow, and let them develop naturally over time.

With work friendships there are boundaries that you may want to maintain and elements of your life that you may not want to expose to office gossip. If you have a safe-for-work social media account that you keep for newer or more professional connections, fine. Otherwise respond to follow requests from colleagues or supervisors with a great deal of caution (or a simple "Thanks, but I have a no social media policy"). Remember, too, that if for any reason your new job doesn't work out, it might mean a big change in those friendships. Be sure to cultivate friendships beyond work so you're not left high and dry if you do end up leaving.

Dressing for Work Without Breaking the Bank

Even if you work someplace with a relaxed office atmosphere, the cost of clothing may still be a concern. A casual look can come with a high price tag. And there will be times you'll want to spiff up your look even in a less-dressy workplace. If you're like many people just starting out in their careers, your salary may not keep up with the expectation your employer has of being professionally dressed. It can get very expensive if you work someplace where you have to suit up on a daily basis.

When you've finally landed that first "real" job, you may be tempted to splurge on the clothes to match. You might do better to get one or two outfits that you feel confident in for your first few days and then take some time to see what your coworkers are wearing on a daily basis. Add pieces one or two at a time in the weeks and months to come. Once you've been at your new job for a bit, you'll have a better sense for what the dress code expectations actually are. Then you can take the time to choose your wardrobe carefully and economically.

Dress codes can vary widely in different parts of the country and from industry to industry. Here are a few universal tips that can help you save money and dress well and wisely no matter where you are or what job you're doing.

1. Focus on high-quality classic pieces as your main wardrobe staples. Unless you're working in the fashion industry (and sometimes even then), you can save money by using accessories as your trendy pieces and sticking to more conservative choices for suits, jackets, pants, or skirts.

2. Choose separates over suits and look for pieces that you

can mix and match. If you have to wear a suit every day, be sure to buy shirts and accessories that can be worn with most suits.

3. Don't be afraid to buy secondhand. There's a learning curve to buying preowned clothing, whether you're looking online or in brick-and-mortar consignment shops and thrift stores, but you can save thousands of dollars a year. It's also nice to know that you're not adding to the throwaway culture and consuming more than necessary.

4. Try to simplify. There are both men's and women's versions of the French wardrobe, a minimalist or capsule wardrobe that uses a limited number of basic pieces.

5. Clear your closet. Donate things you no longer wear and clothes that don't fit. Then you'll know what you actually have and what you still need.

6. Especially if you have to be fashion conscious for your work, think about tapping into the sharing economy. Wardrobe rental companies (Rent the Runway and some designers) allow you to rent high-end clothing instead of having to buy outside your budget. You can also extend your own wardrobe and help a friend if you find a same-size buddy to share and swap pieces with.

7. If you hate to shop or you just can't seem to find things you feel good in, find yourself a real-life or online fashion guru. Look for someone with a similar body type to yours and whose sense of style is a good match for your work life.

TWENTYSOMETHING TALK

A stylist told me to create Pinterest boards of clothes I like for different seasons or reasons. That way when I am shopping I have good ideas of what I want and can focus on finding that style but at a cheaper price point. One final thing is thinking about price per wear. Some things are worth the investment if you'll get a lot of wear and would be an investment piece. —Vicky

NOW DO THIS: What's your next career move? A job? A better job? More responsibility at work? Changing your role at your current job? Identify the next step and take it.

YOU ACTUALLY NEED TO KNOW: In a new job you're learning every day. It can be exhausting. Give yourself credit for the hard work you're doing. Forgive yourself for mistakes. Know that before long what's really challenging now will soon become second nature.

BAD BOSS BINGO

How bad is your bad boss?

takes credit for your work	constantly interrupts you	chatty only when you have a deadline	meeting that could've been an email	doesn't bother to learn your name
increased workload, no raise	pizza party instead of a raise	company outing for management only	Hawaiian shirt day!	puts off vital, time-sensitive decisions
decision took months, changes their mind	"You're doing it wrong" when they don't know how to do it	FREE SPACE	thinks work-life balance is a myth	tries to tell you how to vote
SENDS SHOUTY EMAILS	hoards information	can't/won't delegate	communicates poorly	"You're doing a great job" but doesn't trust you
talks trash about everyone to everyone	refuses to address conflict	hits "Reply all" unnecessarily	bad breath, close talker	throws people under the bus to save their own neck

CHAPTER 3

MY PLACE

Apartment Hunting and Apartment Dwelling

TWENTYSOMETHING TIP: Home may not be heaven, but it should at least be a haven—a safe and comfortable place to return to after being out in the world. You can overcome some of the most common problems renters face by knowing what to look for in an apartment and knowing your rights and responsibilities as a tenant.

What can you afford to spend on your housing?
Though it certainly isn't the only important factor, the number you come up with will influence every other decision about your living space. Knowing how much you can spend will help you decide whether you should live with roommates or housemates and how many, what neighborhoods you should look in, and what kinds of things you might need to compromise on. There are other things to consider, too, as you begin your search. If you'll have a car, is there parking? If you'll be using public transportation, how is the access? In either case, how long of a commute do you think you can manage? Shop around online a bit before you begin looking at places in earnest. That will give you an idea of how much people are paying in which neighborhoods for what amount of space and convenience. Start writing down your preferences and keep a list of questions to ask potential landlords.

Let's Talk Money

The standard advice is to spend no more than one third of your income on housing. In fact, many apartment complexes enforce this as a rule and will not approve your application unless you can prove that you're earning triple the rent you plan to pay. So for an apartment that costs $1,000 a month, you would need to present evidence that you make at least $3,000 monthly or have a cosigner who does. With other expenses continually rising, though, some experts suggest that one quarter of your income would be a more realistic guideline.[1] It's a simple enough calculation, but remember that you'll also need to provide a security deposit (usually equal to one month's rent) before you move in, along with your first month's rent and, in some places, your last month's rent as well.

Make sure you add up all the related expenses. Does the rent include heat, hot water, electricity, and garbage pickup? Is there air conditioning, a laundry facility? If you're renting a house, is there snow removal or lawn care? If you have a car, is there parking, and do you have to pay extra for it? If you have roommates, is there enough parking for all of you? Plan on getting renter's insurance (some landlords require it). It protects the contents of your apartment and provides liability coverage for personal injury. Some apartment-related costs might seem incidental but can add up. If you have a dog or cat, be prepared to pay their rent on top of yours. Most rentals (if they allow pets at all) require an extra hundred dollars or so for a "pet deposit" as well as a higher rent payment every month—sometimes only an additional ten dollars but often fifty dollars or more.

TWENTYSOMETHING TALK

If the option is available, talk with other tenants! Learn about the landlord or management company or maintenance staff and whether they help their tenants out, and learn about the building. Ask about noise, crime, pests (I once found a dead bat in my bathroom), parking (and plowing if you're in a snowy area), mail, garbage, all the things you may have taken for granted in a dorm or with your family. And always ask for a utility estimate and know that you can contact utility companies for the average utility bill. A great deal on an apartment could be totally negated with absurd utility bills if the apartment is drafty or there are other lights/appliances connected to your apartment. —Ryan

Step one, in my opinion, is challenging our own ideas of what a "safe" neighborhood is. Not predominantly white does not equal unsafe, but it is usually more affordable. I had a gorgeous place in Brooklyn three blocks from the subway for half the cost of the nearby trendy neighborhoods. —Taylor

What if you can't afford all this? Don't give up hope. If getting out on your own is a priority or an imperative, you've got several options. If you had planned on living alone consider sharing an apartment with one or more roommates. You could look into a higher-paying job or get a second job. You could compromise on the amount of space you want or the neighborhood you'd like to live in. You may want to rent a room rather than a whole apartment, at least temporarily. Or you may be able to cut costs somewhere else so you can put more of your income toward your housing budget.

Your Own Place or a Shared Space?

Living alone is hard. Sharing your living space with people is also hard. They're each hard in different ways but either option can be the right one for you. If you choose to live on your own, you get to make all the decisions and keep everything just how you want it. You never have to clean up anybody else's mess. You can have quiet whenever you need it or turn the music up when you feel like it. Nobody eats your food or drinks your coffee. You never have to put up with another person's annoying habits. You can have guests whenever you want, and you can watch whatever movie you want whenever you want because nobody else is ever using the TV. On the other hand, you have to make all the decisions and do all the things on your own. Nobody's ever around to help you move the couch, pick out a movie to watch, or make the popcorn. No one lets you have their leftovers from when they went out to lunch. Nobody pays half your bills. And, honestly, it can be lonely and sometimes a little scary being all by yourself.

If you choose to share an apartment with someone else, anyone else—friend, sibling, stranger, or romantic partner—the most obvious benefit is financial. You've got somebody not only to help with your rent but also to split your internet bill or loan you their toothpaste when you run out. You've got somebody to help you move the couch. Other people can be weird and wonderful, and you get to know someone in a unique way when you share a home. If you have a roommate, you know there's always going to be someone on your team when things go bump in the night. Sure, it's *probably* just a stray cat tipping a rake over onto your garbage can, but it *could* be the start of the zombie apocalypse. And, really, who wants to face a horde of zombies alone?

But sometimes that other person doesn't want to help you move the couch. Sometimes that other person doesn't want you to move the couch at all because they like it right where it is. Compromise can be tough, and living with somebody else requires a bunch of it. Other people can be weird and difficult . . . and you never get to know someone else the same way you get to know them when you share a home. Check out chapter 5 for more on the "how to" of living with other people.

Love and Living Space

Do you and your significant other each have your own place but spend all your time at one apartment or the other? It might feel like you're wasting a ton of money by not giving up the second place. Or maybe there's no privacy where you're living now or tension with other roommates about visitors. It's worth considering getting one place for the two of you. But don't leap without looking when it comes to moving in together. It's not just that moving in together can be a big deal; it's more that moving out afterward can be. Nobody moves in together planning to break up, but take time to think and talk through what you would do if it happened.

There are three potential problems ahead:

1. You break up but have to keep living together because neither of you has another place to go (or both of you want the apartment).
2. You break up and one of you moves out but you're both on the lease and the other can't afford the apartment alone.
3. You want to break up but stay in the relationship, at least in part, because living together makes breaking up so much harder.

Try to leave yourself some options in case it doesn't work out. Discuss in advance what will happen if you break up. Find an "Agreement Covering Rented Living Space" or a "Living Together Contract" online, edit it to reflect your agreement, and sign it. Make a copy. Keep it with your lease.

Where and How to Look

The internet provides so many ways to look for real estate that the options can make you dizzy. Craigslist is a great place to start, but there are also many reliable websites (some general real estate sites, others specializing in rentals) that offer nationwide searches, and many have smartphone apps to make the search even easier. Most local newspapers have their old-fashioned classified ads available online now. Consider using a broker or real estate agent if:

- you're looking for space in a big city or a popular neighborhood
- you have very specific needs or special circumstances (physical or health challenges or a complex schedule) that make viewing every apartment difficult
- you're relocating from a distance and won't be on-site until you move
- the thought of making phone calls and setting up showings makes you want to hide under a rock

You might pay a one-time fee (most commonly one month's rent, but this varies widely) in exchange for helping you find a place; sometimes the landlord pays the fee to the agent for finding a good tenant.

Unless you have a reason to keep your moving plans quiet, it often helps to spread the word among your friends, family, and colleagues that you're looking for a place. Take a look through your contacts and see if anyone you know (or anyone they know) lives near where you're headed. They may have advice on where and how best to find a place. There may be local resources or informal connections that you can access by using your networks.

How to Spot a Shady Deal

The best way to protect yourself from an unscrupulous landlord is to know your rights and get familiar with local standard practices. You've probably heard the saying "If it seems too good to be true, it probably is." Have you got a friend or relative who's always a little suspicious of everyone and everything? Bring that person along when you look at apartments. If you are either excited or desperate to move, it's good to have a skeptic on your team.

If anyone wants money from you for anything other than rent or a security deposit, or if someone wants you to pay cash instead of writing a check, doesn't want to show you the entire apartment, or won't let you bring someone with you to see the apartment, those are red flags. If you're asked to provide your social security number and date of birth and pay an application fee "to run a credit check" before even receiving the address, that apartment may not exist.

If you're promised something fabulous for a relatively small amount of money, be suspicious. If there is something unusual in the lease, if you're asked to sign away any of your legal rights as a tenant (which is illegal, by the way), or if they want you to agree to ignore any of their responsibilities as a landlord, your answer is no. If you get a bad feeling about the building, the neighbors, the neighborhood, the landlord, or the lease, find out why it's so cheap before you sign anything. Search online for reviews of the building or apartment complex, the landlord, or the management company; if you can, talk to previous tenants or people around the neighborhood.

A Landlord You Can Trust

A good or bad landlord can really make or break a housing situation, no matter how great or terrible the apartment is. And just like with everybody else, you can think you have a good feel for a landlord and still be surprised, for better or worse. Checking out the landlord before you sign a lease is a great idea. You can ask for references from current or former tenants or do your own investigating. Ask the neighbors what they know or check your local Fair Housing Board, the Better Business Bureau, or your state's landlord association.

TWENTYSOMETHING TALK

Finding a trusty landlord is a needle in a haystack, a miracle, a godsend. Landlords ask for tenant references; so should you ask for landlord references. —Jennifer

Ask about the last service dates on the furnace, water heater, and roof and how old the windows are. Older furnaces, water heaters, and windows can jack up your utilities even if you're doing everything right. —Ryan

There are things landlords can't legally ask you, and if they do anyway, they probably aren't great at following other rules, like rules about when to address your broken window. These mostly involve questions about race, gender, religion, age, and sexual orientation—but they vary by location. Your state or local government should spell everything out online.

In most states, your landlord is legally required to:

- comply with local health and safety codes
- keep all common areas clean and safe

- provide running water
- perform all necessary repairs
- provide proper trash bins

If you believe that there is a health or safety violation, your first step is to contact your landlord. Keep a record of the communication, including the date. If the problem is not fixed within a reasonable period of time (the legal time frame varies by state), then you should complain to the department of health and public safety. But since your lease is a legal contract, your landlord is responsible for doing everything stated on your lease.

Here are some tips for getting what you're entitled to before, during, and after your tenancy.

Before You Move In . . .

1. **Get it in writing.** Make sure your lease spells out every single thing (beyond legal obligations) that you are responsible for and everything your landlord is responsible for. Write an addendum to the lease if necessary. Ask questions and write down the answers.

2. **Organize.** Get a file box or other safe place to keep your lease, and keep it updated with dated copies of every single communication you have with your landlord. Your landlord might go back on their word, change their mind, or simply forget what you agreed on. Back everything up with digital copies, even if it's just a photograph of the paper copy.

TWENTYSOMETHING TALK

Take pictures before you move your stuff in. Be especially careful to document chips, cracks, dents, holes, etc. A rental experience bit me in the butt, taking over half our deposit for normal wear and tear and damage not from us. I couldn't take off time from work to fight it in small claims and was going through a managing company for the actual landlord. Not a fun learning experience. —Amanda

While You Live There . . .

1. **Keep documenting everything.** Keep a record of what you discussed in your phone calls. If one call doesn't do the trick, send emails (which are automatically date stamped) or certified letters asking for things to be fixed. Get rent receipts to prove that you paid on time.

2. **Let your money talk.** If you are thinking of withholding rent over a violation, be absolutely certain your situation meets the legal requirements for this. Keep the withheld money in a bank account and keep copies of your bank statements so you can prove you intended to pay it as soon as the situation was resolved.

When You Move Out . . .

1. **Keep records.** If your landlord sends you a letter or tells you verbally what you're expected to do (cleaning, etc.) before you vacate, keep that information handy. If you

receive a letter afterward (with or without part of your security deposit), keep it.

2. **Take photos.** Thoroughly document the condition of the apartment when you left it.

3. **Do a walk-through.** If possible, do a walk-through with the landlord (and take a video) after you have removed all your belongings. If either of you notes any damage, you can discuss whether it was there when you moved in, whether it is normal wear and tear, or what fee will be deducted from your security deposit for its repair.

4. **Wait a minute.** If your landlord eventually returns part but not all of your security deposit and you think you are entitled to more, wait before you cash the check. Reply in writing that you dispute the amount and keep a copy of your reply. In some states cashing the check means you have legally accepted that amount of money as all that you are entitled to.

TWENTYSOMETHING TALK

Know your rights. There are landlords out there who will take your security deposit for things they are not legally allowed to. —Haddie

I Can't Live Here

Sometimes, despite your best efforts, you find yourself in a living situation that just isn't livable. Maybe you have an issue with your landlord, your neighbors, your cotenants, or your apartment itself that you simply can't get worked out. Your options at this point may be somewhat limited, but you do still have options.

There should be a clause in your lease detailing the procedures and penalties for breaking your lease. Look for words like "sublet," "early release," and "re-rent." It's always best to have a refresher on what you agreed to before you approach your landlord, but that should be your very next step.

If you feel you need to leave the apartment right away because *of* your landlord, then hopefully you've already been in negotiations, and it should not come as a total shock. If you need to move out for any other reason, like job loss or relocation, for instance, then your landlord will appreciate as much notice as possible. An apartment often loses at least one month of rental income by changing tenants, and your landlord may have to take the time to go through the process of listing and showing the apartment, screening applicants, running credit checks, collecting deposits, and signing a new lease, so the more notice the better.

Subletting

If your lease or your landlord allows, you can find someone else to rent your apartment to. Your landlord will still have the right to approve your tenant or not and will hold on to your security deposit until the lease is up and the new tenant either signs a new lease (at which point you are free and clear) or moves out (at which point you are free and clear). You will still be responsible for any damage, and, depending on your agreement with the landlord, you may be responsible for collecting the rent and paying the landlord. If the landlord is willing to collect the rent from your sublessee, you will still be liable if that person doesn't pay. You may have to offer an incentive (like reducing the rent payment for the new tenant and covering the balance yourself) in order to avoid losing even more money, damaging your rental history and credit rating, or possibly even being subject to legal action by breaking your lease.

Re-renting

Re-renting involves finding a new tenant for the unit (whether it's done by you or by the landlord), but instead of taking over and finishing out your lease, the new tenant will start a lease of their own and pay their own security deposit, and you will be free and clear. Re-renting allows the landlord to "mitigate damages" by losing less money (or even no money) due to the early termination of your lease. The less money the landlord loses, the less money they are likely to charge you.

Breaking Your Lease

If your landlord is not willing to allow a sublet, if you are unable to find a new renter, or if you're in a situation where you need to leave the apartment immediately, you may need to break your lease. A lease is a legal contract, so in order to break that contract without serious repercussions, you need to have a good reason. If you don't have a reason that your landlord or a court of law considers acceptable, you may need to comply with the termination offer detailed in your lease. This will probably entail a hefty fee, possibly as much as two months' rent and your security deposit.

. . . .

Acceptable legal reasons vary between states, but your landlord should be willing to voluntarily release you from your rental contract due to military deployment, medical need, or a domestic violence situation. You should also be released from the contract if the landlord fails to maintain a habitable property (has running water and is free of health and safety risks) or illegally enters the property, but you may need to go to court to make this happen.

A Renter's Rights and Responsibilities

Responsibilities: As the tenant you are responsible for . . .

- paying your rent on time
- paying your utilities (if not included in rent) on time
- abiding by the terms of your lease
- protecting the property from damage due to negligence
- keeping records of agreements/arrangements made between you and your landlord
- handling your relationships with any roommates or

romantic partners so that they don't cause an issue with the landlord or neighbors

- alerting your landlord to any situations or repairs that require their attention
- communicating your plans for moving out, adding a tenant, or (in extreme situations) withholding rent

Rights: As the tenant you have the right to . . .

- a habitable space (must have running water and be free of health and safety hazards)
- prompt repairs, if anything breaks
- privacy—your landlord may not enter without at least twenty-four hours' notice except in cases of emergency[2]
- be notified of any health concerns (mold, pests) and have them handled promptly and appropriately
- anything and everything else that your lease specifies is included in your rent

Variants by state and city: Your state's laws are available online. Your city may have additional requirements that may also be posted. See if your community has a fair housing board. Such groups are usually nonprofits or government organizations set up to help people understand their housing rights. If no such group is available and you have questions about your local housing laws, you can consult a tenants' union, renters' rights group, local housing authority, legal aid, or lawyer.

To learn more and to find answers to frequently asked questions, search for your state, city, or county and "tenants' rights" (the result you're looking for will likely end in .gov).

What to Bring When Signing Your Lease

- — **driver's license** or other government-issued photo ID
- — **pay stubs,** and if you have no rental history, no credit history, or not-so-great credit, also be ready to show proof of your employment history
- — **bank statements** from at least one bank account, preferably two (both checking and savings)
- — **a qualified cosigner** if you have one, and their photo ID, pay stubs, bank statements
- — **vehicle registration and insurance** if you have a car that will be parked on the premises
- — **your checkbook** or another way to pay whatever money is due at signing

TWENTYSOMETHING TALK

A *huge* thing about living on your own is that you need to get to know your rights as a tenant. These are different in every state, and sometimes cities can even differ. Learn what you can and can't do and when you have the right to withhold your rent (e.g., you haven't had running water for three days). It'll save you time and arguments with your landlord. —Falon

---

NOW DO THIS: Have you got a copy of your lease? Do you have your landlord's phone number? Do you have a spare key? Give one to a friend or keep it in your desk at work in case you ever get locked out or yours gets misplaced or stolen.

YOU ACTUALLY NEED TO KNOW: A little bit of know-how can go a long way when it comes to getting what you need in your living space.

CHAPTER 4

ADULTING AT YOUR PARENTS' HOUSE

TWENTYSOMETHING TIP: Living with your parents, whether by choice or necessity, doesn't have to mean putting off your adulthood. There are steps you can take to move toward greater independence at the same time you're enjoying the positives (and navigating the challenges) of living at home.

For some people it's a cultural thing. For many it's a practical thing. Whatever the reason you find yourself home again (or still), there are some serious benefits to living with family as a twentysomething. Or maybe you're living on your own now but contemplating a move back home. It's not without its problems, but very often the positives can outweigh the downsides. Being in a familiar place with familiar people, not to mention how much less it usually costs, can make living with parents a really great choice for a lot of people. That's why 55 percent of people between the ages of eighteen and twenty-four live in their parents' home.[1] The stability, reliability, and savings make it a hard choice to pass up.

Communication and Expectations

Some families move through challenging times with a spirit of cooperation and mutual support. Others, not so much. Even if your family has not always been great at communicating, you can change that dynamic, or at least influence it, by changing your approach. Positive communication is "respectful, open, honest, straightforward, and kind," according to experts at Michigan State University.[2] Wherever your family falls on the "Let's talk this over calmly" spectrum, know that by holding to the ideals of positive communication, you can help. Positive communication includes talking about problems before they become arguments. It means expressing appreciation as well as talking about points of tension. In the same way you would talk with roommates about household concerns, talk with your family. Obviously, communication can be more complex with family because these are people you're related to. There's inevitably baggage that goes along with that. Do your best to step back from the family history and come at any conflict with a cool head and your adult communication skills.

Knowing what is expected of you can go a long way toward avoiding conflict in the first place. Of course, you'll want to have a conversation about financial expectations, but talk as well about all the other typical points of conflict:

1. **Coming and going.** Talk about when you'll be home and when you won't. In the same way you would let a roommate or housemate know when you plan to be around for shared meals or if you plan to be out late or gone overnight, let your family know. Not so they can tell you what to do but out of consideration.

2. **Projects and priorities.** Is there a family calendar? If there are family events you're expected to attend or projects your family wants or needs your help with, ask for some advance notice. In turn, let them know if you're planning a big weekend away or if you'll

have work or other demands that will keep you from participating.

3. **Cleaning the commons.** Expect to do your share to keep common areas in order and to be a considerate housemate. Ask ahead of time what's expected and try to get as specific as possible. See if there's a particular task (or set of tasks) you could take on that could be your contribution. If there are chores that everyone takes a turn at, be sure you're on that rotation regularly. Clean up after yourself and be considerate about how you keep your own space. If you're doing your own laundry, make sure you include a load of household laundry occasionally (towels, sheets, etc.). If clothes are washed in common, take your turn handling those responsibilities.

4. **Cooking conversations.** If the family eats together frequently, have a conversation about taking your turn putting the meal together regularly. If you're not ready to take on preparing a meal for the whole crew, now is a good time to apprentice yourself to the person who does that in your family and learn how.

5. **Calming conflict.** Whenever possible, stay out of disagreements between your parents and siblings. Offering private sympathy and gentle advice to a sibling you get along with might help calm some family conflict, but jumping into an argument and siding with one party or the other is sure to come back to bite you. Don't rise to the bait if there are siblings around who try to aggravate

you. Keep calm and remove yourself from any situation you can't keep your cool in.

6. **Can we talk?** It can be weird to talk with your parents as an adult about your choices around drinking, smoking/vaping, sex, or other things that might not have had their approval when you were underage. Be as honest as you can about your choices and deal with things aboveboard whenever possible. It gets tricky when the people who raised you are now your landlords and housemates. You are an autonomous person but living in their space. They have a legitimate voice concerning anything that takes place in their house. If there are choices you make that they disapprove of, those activities might need to take place somewhere else.

7. **Checking in.** Be in the habit of asking questions like: Is there anything I can do? Is everything going okay? Is there anything that I'm doing or not doing that's bothering you? Don't be afraid to talk about what you need and want too. Listen and be open. Try not to be defensive, and seek compromise whenever possible.

TWENTYSOMETHING TALK

If you need to live with family, be sure to talk about expectations and communicate often; anything from what chores are expected, whether you're covering any expenses, if everyone will be eating dinner together, any house rules, whether you can invite friends over and what that looks like, any quiet hours, dishes policy, pet peeves, what spaces are shared, etc. The best thing about living with family is that you get to bond and spend more time with them, but sometimes that makes it hard to talk if something about their habits is annoying you. —Jamie

Backsliding

Being around family can be great. The familiarity of it can be a comfort and even a confidence booster. But being back home brings with it the danger of sliding back into habits we had when we were younger. Especially if there are habits you've kicked since the last time you lived at home, keep an eye on your own behavior. Don't let the familiar surroundings drag you into a behavior that you've overcome or that you're trying to beat. Check out chapter 12 for more on habits.

Moving Toward Financial Independence

Talk with your parent(s) about your financial goals. You may want to put most of your income toward paying down your debt. Or your priority right now might be saving enough money to move out. Let them know what you're hoping to accomplish in the near future. It might figure into whether and how much they want you to contribute toward household expenses. If they do want you to pay rent, discuss what that amount should be in light of your goals. If you have the kind of parents with whom you can safely share your fears and concerns along with your hopes, you can probably just talk that through together.

If your relationship with your folks around money is a little more strained, look at your own budget ahead of time so you can confidently enter into that conversation knowing you are making reasonable requests. That said, parents are often eager to give financial advice. Inviting them to offer you theirs (even if you don't take it) can allay some of the concerns they may have on your behalf. It's not so much a matter of doing what they tell you as it is taking their advice into consideration.

Even if you're contributing financially toward room and board, it's usually considerably less than you'd pay for an equal amount of benefits out in the world. If you've never had to make it on your own, ask your parents to help you track the hidden expenses you need to be aware of, and use that information to develop a budget for when you get your own place. Look at chapters 3 and 8 and think about all of the expenses you'd have if you weren't living at home. Resist the temptation to live beyond your means right now. Save rather than spend. That doesn't mean you have to live like a hermit. You can still go out and do the things you like to do, but a little frugality is both good practice and can help you avoid criticism from anyone watching that you're not being responsible.

Agreeing to Disagree

Disagreements about things like values, politics, and religion can be some of the biggest points of tension between adult children and their parents. Living in the same house can make those tensions flare up into all-out battles. How can you live with people you fundamentally disagree with without feeling like you've sold out? Here are four approaches to consider:

1. Be respectful. When it comes to the things you cannot agree on, be as diplomatic as you can.
2. Remember that people are more than their beliefs. People in your life who you love and who care about you may have different perspectives. Just by being in their lives you may help expand their thinking.
3. Understand that your parents have come to their beliefs through their own experiences. Try to keep in mind that they grew up in a different time. They've seen things you haven't (just as you've seen things they haven't). Feel free to share your experience, but don't be too disappointed if they don't understand your thinking. At least not right away.
4. Once you've agreed to disagree, leave it alone. If there's a hot topic that keeps coming up, don't be afraid to say (in your own words), "This is what I believe. When you consistently say these things in front of me, I feel like _____." Fill in that blank with whatever is true for your situation: you don't respect me, you want to have a disagreement, you don't care about my feelings or beliefs, etc.

These kinds of disagreements are hard. *Really* hard. You have to weigh the importance of those disagreements against having a roof over your head.

TWENTYSOMETHING TALK

Have a sanctuary and your own life outside of the family drama. Make it a point to meet up with friends, have a hobby, work out—anything to make you feel like yourself. —Zahrah

How to Have Boundaries

Learning to stick up for yourself with your family can be a big challenge. If you have people in your family who are emotionally manipulative or who don't recognize other people's needs, one of the best things you can do for your own well-being is to learn about boundaries. It can be uncomfortable saying no when you'd rather keep the peace. Do you end up as the automatic babysitter, cleanup crew, chauffeur, house sitter, pet care person, or family errand runner? Are demands being made over and above what you've agreed to as part of your family contribution? Do you feel like you're not allowed to say no to these extras? It's fine to just get along some of the time, but if you start to notice that you're not allowed to make your own choices or you constantly feel that you're not doing the things that are important to you, pay attention to that. Learn to ask for what you need and to stand up for yourself with your family. That's part of becoming an adult too. Building the skills to help you stand your ground will serve you well now and for the rest of your life.

If you have family members who take advantage of your good will or are just openly manipulative, try some of these tactics:

1. Learn to recognize when you're being manipulated or guilted into helping. Other people's problems are not yours to solve, but a true narcissist will try to make you feel like they are. If you choose to help or make yourself available, be sure it's actually what you want to do.
2. Anticipate requests (or assumptions) and alert folks that you have other things to do (time for yourself counts). Tell them you have plans and stick to your guns.
3. Avoid being the backup/safety plan, especially if you know they won't look for other solutions if *they know* they have you to fall back on.

TWENTYSOMETHING TALK

I'm forever grateful my parents took me in after college. I saved so much money! What saved me was keeping busy with a full-time job and lots of extra activities that kept me active in the community. My parents treated me more like an adult, too, because I finished college and then worked full-time. I have pretty awesome parents. —April

NOW DO THIS: Review this chapter and chapter 9 and choose one positive step to take to move from kid status to grown-up status with your family.

YOU ACTUALLY NEED TO KNOW: If you were "away" at college and now you're back home for a while, it can be especially style cramping. Don't just settle into old patterns; forge a new relationship with your family that respects everyone's new roles.

PART 2

THE BASICS OF TWENTY-SOMETHING LIFE

CHAPTER 5

SHARED SPACES VS. SOLITARY PLACES

Roommates, House Rules, and
Cleaning Routines

TWENTYSOMETHING TIP: Life with roommates
can be hard, but there are some big benefits
that come along with having a home crew. Living
on your own can be lonelier but simpler. Weigh
your options, figure out what's best for you, and
then create a home you like coming home to.

Maybe you're an off-the-charts extrovert and already know that you need people around to survive. Perhaps you are more of an introvert and get energized by solitude. Those are important factors as you make choices about your living situation. There are other considerations that might overrule preferences, though, when it comes to where you live and with whom. Factors like how much you can afford, safety, commuting distance, and transportation options will all play a role in the choices you make about your living situation. But whether you're alone or with a group, you can make your living situation work for you.

Shared Spaces

If you've shared space before, then you already know that life is easier and a whole lot more pleasant if you can get along with the people you're living with. People can have shockingly different expectations when it comes to things like cleanliness, noise, smoking/vaping, overnight guests, pets, and more. Definitely plan to have those conversations before you commit to living with a person or people, and find out how much common ground you have.

More important than finding people you already agree with on those things is finding people you can talk to and compromise with. If you've got time and options, look for roommates who are good communicators and who have a measure of kindness. As you rank potential housemates, give bonus points to candidates whose former roommates still have a friendly relationship with them. If your options are limited or you're moving in with people you don't know well, establish good communication early on by asking questions about common conflict causers (see our list later in the chapter) and expressing your own preferences about the things that matter most to you.

Finding Roommates

Some people are comfortable finding their new roommates online and living with strangers. Others wouldn't dream of doing that and will only live with people they are already friends with. Still others rely on friends to connect them with people they know who are also looking for roommates. The approach you choose really depends on what you're comfortable with. None of these approaches guarantees success (or failure). It's up to you to choose the approach that sounds best for you.

TWENTYSOMETHING TALK

My roommate is my best friend from high school. We got a two-bedroom apartment. I don't remember how we decided who got the bigger room, but I ended up with it. Whenever we have a conflict we both take about twenty minutes to do whatever we need to do to calm down—she tends to take a walk, and I just tend to need a few minutes alone. It really helps us gather our thoughts so we can come back and be honest and get points across to each other without saying something we don't mean. —Cat

As someone who lives in an expensive city, I've found almost all my roommates through Craigslist (and it has worked out very well). We basically conduct mini job interviews for potential roommates, asking about the things that matter to us (cleanliness, conflict management / communication, schedules, what they're looking for in a roommate, etc.). And, having lived with the same Craigslist-found person for over three years, we try to address anything that might irritate us before we're actually upset and set up household guidelines to help (like splitting chores so each person does what they're most sensitive about). The largest room goes to the person who's willing to pay more. Compromise! Assume good intentions from others and remember that what might seem obvious or rude to you may completely not register that way to someone else. Really, communication is at the root of so much. —Bridget

I reached out to a contact in the young adult group at the church I planned on attending to see if any other women were looking for a roommate. I found the best housemate ever! We both split chores and would share occasional meals together. We attended mass together when our schedules allowed and made sure to do things around town together and with our mutual friends when each of our busy schedules aligned. —DeAnna

For every person who has found a good match—through any approach—there are also horror stories. Living with friends can be great because it's a known quantity. Presumably, you already know their strengths and weaknesses and whether or not those qualities will be a good match with your strengths and weaknesses. On the downside, if it goes wrong, you don't just need to find a new living situation—you might need to find new friends. If you do choose to share your living space with friends, be just as rigorous with establishing house rules and cleaning agreements as you would be with strangers. If your boundaries get crossed, speak up sooner rather than later.

Rent is often divided equally in situations where the bedrooms are all about the same. If there's a big difference in size or quality of the rooms (there's a master bedroom or a bedroom without a window; one with more privacy in the basement or one next to a noisy stairwell), expect those differences to be reflected in the total amount each person pays for rent. See chapter 3 for details on who goes on the lease and what your responsibilities are if it's you.

TWENTYSOMETHING TALK

For five grad student young women sharing a five-bedroom house, we literally drew numbers out of a hat for who got to pick their room in which order. Just dumb luck, and we all agreed on it, and it was fair.
—Ann

Common Conflict Causers

These are some of the top causes of conflict between roommates, but you may have specific concerns like allergies, safety, or others that you'll want to address ahead of time.

1. **Will overnight guests be allowed?** How many guests is too many? How many nights is too many? Can the guest have the couch or should they be in the bedroom of the person who invited them?

2. **Is smoking and drinking permitted?** Will you allow vaping/cigarette smoking, pot smoking, drinking in the apartment?

3. **How can you respect each other's sleep schedules?** Do you work nights and need quiet during the day to sleep? What times would be good to consider quiet hours in the apartment?

4. **Who is responsible for which chores?** Besides each person cleaning up after themselves, who will do what cleaning and how often? Is a chore chart needed or can people be counted on to remember to do their part?

5. **Who will handle which bills?** By what day of the month does the person handling the bills need everyone's share?

6. **How are you divvying up food?** Will food in the fridge be communal or does what each person buys individually belong only to them? If food is communal, who does the shopping?

7. **Will pets be allowed?** Small, caged, or none at all? How many is too many? Who will take care of them?

8. **What counts as acceptable cleanliness?** Consider both household and personal cleanliness. Three days of unwashed dishes sitting in the sink or three days of unwashed house-mate sitting on the couch are equally likely to be deal breakers for many people!

Clever Cleaning Tricks for People Who Hate to Clean

Learning to take some time, even just a little, every day to put your stuff in order can have big benefits.

1. **Tackle one gross thing.** If you're not a habitual cleaner, the grossness can quickly get out of hand. Try doing one gross thing a day. Pick a time of day, maybe right when you get home from work or just before bed, and do one short cleanup job, five minutes or less. Wipe down the bathroom mirror, pick up all the trash from your room, or scoop all the dirty socks out from under your bed. Stay on task and don't let it balloon into a bigger job. Just do one gross thing. Do a different one every day. It might become a habit.

2. **Set a timer.** Even if you hate to clean, you can stand almost anything for ten or fifteen minutes. Choose a room, set a timer, and go! It can be surprising how much you can get done.

3. **Clean up by category.** If you've got to clean a whole room

and find that daunting, divide the job up by categories—
first pick up all the trash, then get all the dirty dishes
to the sink. Next get all clothes picked up. Then stack
papers and books.

4. **Clean as you go.** Get in the habit of cleaning up while
you cook and putting things away as soon as you finish
using them. If you clear the table and do the dishes as soon
as you finish eating, you're doing your future self a favor.
Even though we tell ourselves we'll feel more like doing an
unpleasant task later, the hard fact is that if you don't feel
like doing it now, you probably won't feel like doing it then.

5. **Multitask.** Fold laundry while you watch TV. Wash the
dishes while you talk on the phone. Sweep or vacuum
with earbuds in and music or your favorite podcast playing. Pairing an unpleasant task with an enjoyable activity
can reduce your resistance to it.

Cleaning Supplies Checklist

You don't need to spend a lot of money to keep your place clean.
You'll pay more for convenience when it comes to cleaning
supplies. For speed and ease you can buy brand-name convenience products like Lysol or Clorox wipes and a Swiffer. Or
make your own simple spray cleaner and use rags for almost no
money at all. If you have a big place with hardwood or linoleum
floors, cleaning with a Swiffer is going to get expensive. If you
have a tiny place and the only floor you need to wet clean is the

bathroom, you probably won't want to bother hauling out a mop and bucket for that. Here's a basic list that balances expense with convenience. You can adjust it in either direction as needed:

— broom and dustpan
— vacuum (if you have carpets)
— mop and bucket (if you have floors to wet clean)
— toilet brush
— sponges and scrubby pads
— vinegar dilute to clean glass or counters
— bleach, dilute to sanitize or disinfect
— baking soda as a mild abrasive cleaner and for odor control
— rubbing alcohol—use straight to disinfect or remove ink
— dish soap to dilute and use for general cleaning
— an all-purpose spray cleaner
— paper towels

Other optional items include:

— duster
— microfiber dust cloths
— empty spray bottle to mix your own cleaner
— enzyme spray cleaner if you have pets
— rubber gloves to make gross jobs less gross
— bag of rags (old T-shirts, towels, washcloths, socks)
— cleaning wipes
— Swiffer and pads
— Magic Eraser

If you are new to cleaning, heed these warnings: Never mix ammonia and bleach. Never mix rubbing alcohol and bleach. Read warnings on labels. Ventilate while you clean—some cleaners are toxic. Environmentally friendly is often also human and pet friendly. Some people are allergic to fragrances. Never use an abrasive cleaner on scratchable surfaces.

TWENTYSOMETHING TALK

For cleaning just buy all of the Clorox wipes you can afford, one all-purpose bathroom cleaner, and one thing of Windex for everything else. Also cheap paper towels. —Emma

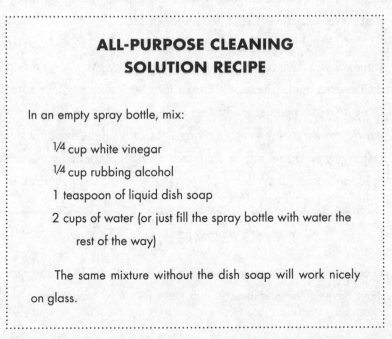

ALL-PURPOSE CLEANING SOLUTION RECIPE

In an empty spray bottle, mix:

¼ cup white vinegar

¼ cup rubbing alcohol

1 teaspoon of liquid dish soap

2 cups of water (or just fill the spray bottle with water the rest of the way)

The same mixture without the dish soap will work nicely on glass.

No Martyrs, No Mind Readers

Can you cheerfully pick up after others? Do you find putting a room in order calming? That can be great, especially if you live with people who lack that disposition and don't mind someone moving their stuff. If you find yourself getting angry or resentful of the mess makers as you clean, though, it might mean that you are morphing into a Martyr. If that happens, it's time to stop and ask them (nicely!) to clean up after themselves.

"No Martyrs" is a good household rule. The Martyr has the attitude, "I'm doing it because nobody else will." The problem with that is it erodes relationships and allows everybody to get away with some pretty bad behavior. The mess makers don't have to clean up after themselves and the Martyr (sometimes selfrighteously) seethes but doesn't voice frustration until the situation is at a breaking point. It's a recipe for disaster.

"No Mind Readers" is another good rule similar to "No Martyrs." It means you have to actually express your thoughts, your likes and dislikes, out loud. The mess that's driving you crazy might be something that the people you live with don't even notice. The person who keeps annoying you by moving your stuff might think they are helping by putting things away. If something is bothering you, speak up! Don't expect that the people you live with can read your mind.

TWENTYSOMETHING TALK

Two big things I would say about conflict: First off, your roommates don't have to be your best friends. You just have to get along and reasonably agree on the tangible stuff—how clean to have the place, where to set the thermostat (surprisingly difficult), overall vibe of noisy/quiet/party/mellow/early/late household. That stuff will mess up a friendship, especially a casual one with people you thought you liked but didn't really know. Second, establish good communication. This is a duh, but it's also the hardest thing. Set clear expectations up front about money (who pays the landlord, when rent is due to the person paying the landlord, what happens if that's not met, very specific expectations about the security deposit). Practice, practice, practice the art of conflict. It takes time to learn how to confront someone about something that's bugging you, in a way that's not super personal, before it gets so bad that you (or they) blow up. Establish healthy boundaries. It's not unreasonable for me to ask my roommates to do x, y, or z. It's not unreasonable for them to ask me to do this or that. Figure out your boundaries and discuss them and practice maintaining them. That's how you build trust without getting pissed off at each other. —Eric

Significant Conversations About Significant Others

Take the time to talk with potential roommates about how you will handle significant others. An extra person who contributes to rent or the food budget, helps with cleaning or cooking, and is pleasant to have around can be a nice addition to your household. But it's not usually that simple. If the significant other is sleeping over more often than not and is in the common spaces frequently or is around when the person they are dating is not home, it's probably time to formalize the relationship. If you've already made agreements with your roommates about overnight guests, then this can be just one more conversation in that same category. Use extra caution if your living arrangement is you and just one other roommate. You can suddenly find yourself out-numbered if your roommate's significant other becomes part of household decision-making.

TWENTYSOMETHING TALK

It's critical to have discussions about significant others. Is everyone on the lease okay if there essentially ends up being an extra roommate because someone's significant other is there 90 percent of the time? If not, how often is too often? Does the presence of a significant other impact bills? Food sharing? I've even known roommate situations (not my own) where things like whether or not a couple was allowed to have sex while the roommate was home led to disaster. With virtually everyone I know the presence of significant others in shared housing might be one of the biggest, but also one of the least-discussed, areas of potential conflict. —Emily

Before You Move In . . .

1. Assess what kind of living situation will be best for you (and your budget).
2. Figure out your preferences vs. your deal breakers.

3. Think ahead about potential problems and how to solve them early.
4. Establish house rules and habits for health and happiness (even if you're living alone).

Once You're There . . .

1. Be aware of pulling your weight as a roommate, and encourage others to do the same.
2. Communicate clearly and kindly (avoid passive-aggressive notes; face-to-face communication is usually best).

Alone but Not Lonely

Whether by choice or by necessity, you may find yourself living alone, possibly for the first time in your life. For the solitude-loving introvert, this can be heaven. Finally, you can choose whether, when, and with whom to interact, in your free time at least. For those who prefer more company, it can take a little time to adjust to living alone. Many twentysomethings struggle at first with living alone. Coming home to an empty apartment when you're used to a busy dorm or family home can take some getting used to. Over time many of those same twentysomethings come to love it. Regardless of your capacity for company, everyone needs to find a healthy balance between living in complete isolation versus never giving yourself a break from other people.

TWENTYSOMETHING TALK

You should always take advantage of the time you have alone because it only happens for a small moment, and you never get it back again. It's a great time to learn things that you don't know how to do or try something you've always wanted to do. —Zahrah

One of the best first things to do if you're living alone is to make your place your own. Don't live out of boxes just because there's no one else around who will see. Instead do what you can with what you have to create a feeling of home and make a space that you want to invite friends into. Next, get into a routine to keep your place (relatively) clean. Then you'll be more likely to actually have friends over, and you can enjoy this haven that's all yours.

Six Tricks for Moving Through Loneliness After You've Moved In

When you're sick of taking refuge in your screens but need to push through homesickness, or if you're feeling antsy or uncomfortable in your new place, try some of these:

1. **Create a day-off list.** Make a list of things you want to get done and fun things to do on your day off so it's not all laundry or lazing around. Fight that feeling that you

wasted your weekend by packing some fun in or getting something accomplished.

2. **Schedule a call.** Plan to catch up with a friend or family member via a real phone call instead of just texting. If you're having a hard time getting through your work week, make it a weekly thing—"Wednesday night is phone call night"—either with the same person or reconnect with a different old friend each week.

3. **Entertain.** It doesn't have to be big or fancy, though it certainly can be, but have people over. Board game night, dish-to-pass dinner, or just a hangout can help you declare your apartment a place you plan to be happy in. There's nothing like food, company, conversation, and laughter to make your space feel like home.

4. **Be a bibliophile.** Build a small comfort library of beloved books, comedy, poetry, photography, travel, or whatever gets you dreaming, reminiscing, or motivated.

5. **Have a project.** Fight the aversion of coming home to a place that doesn't feel like home yet by having a creative project going. Even in a teeny-tiny apartment you can carve out a space to be creative. Fill a box or small suitcase with your supplies and keep it under your bed. Keep a sheet of sturdy cardboard behind your dresser to use as a work surface. If you have the luxury of a little more space, consider providing yourself a setup for your favorite creative effort.

6. **Make things come alive.** Add some living things to your living space. Plants, a fish tank, or other low-maintenance pets can all add a sense of home to a new space.

7. **Schedule guests.** Invite out-of-town friends or family to come stay. Keep an eye out for local events and activities someone you love might enjoy. A music or arts weekend, a foodie event, or a street festival can all be great ways to spend time with the people you're missing while you explore your new surroundings. Make a project out of getting your place ready for them.

TWENTYSOMETHING TALK

Learning to take good care of myself, even when I didn't feel like it, was the hardest part of living alone for me. It was like a little investment in myself for later or for another day—whether that meant buying some nice food or cooking something in advance or even buying myself flowers once in a while rather than feeling sad or wishing I had someone to do that for me. I could do it for myself. It was learning to be empowered. —Debra

Push through the initial discomfort of living on your own with a mixture of toughing it out and taking good care of yourself. Author and advice columnist Harlan Cohen encouraged people to get comfortable with the uncomfortable. "Discomfort is front-loaded," he explained.[1] When you're doing something new, the uncomfortable part is almost always the beginning stage. Get through that and the rest will be easier.

An Epidemic of Loneliness

In 2018 the global health service company Cigna found nearly half of the twenty thousand adults they surveyed sometimes or always feel alone or left out. Generation Z (ages eighteen to twenty-two at that time) and Millennials (twenty-three to thirty-seven) self-reported the highest level of feelings associated with loneliness.[2] There are lots of different reasons that loneliness has become such a big problem; we're a highly mobile society, and work and family patterns have changed dramatically over the course of the last generation. The good news is that the solutions can be pretty simple.

Even if you have roommates, depending on your schedules, you may not be spending much time together. The place you're living can be "just a place to live" and that's a legitimate option. You don't have to socialize with the people you share living space with. A downside to that approach is you might be missing out on one of your best sources of social support. Having social support means you have people who listen to you, care about you, and help you. Not every roommate situation makes for a good social support situation, but it's worth considering whether that's something you're looking for (check out the tips in chapter 10 if you need to build social support in general). If so, know that creating a supportive community with the people you live with doesn't happen automatically. Human beings are complicated, and when you share living space that's doubly true. But with time and intention you can turn the place you stay into more than just a roof overhead. It can be home.

There's a wealth of information online about living arrangements that are more than just a place to stay. They go by names like coliving, intentional community, cohousing, and commune living. Some are formal with legal agreements and long histories. Some are just a handful of people who took the next step beyond being roommates to becoming a supportive community for each other. Here a few steps you could take to move in the direction of creating an intentional community:

1. Do it on purpose (be intentional). Talk about your idea with the people you're living with or planning to live with, or seek out others who have a similar interest.

2. Discover what you have in common and make the most of that. Is everyone interested in service? Or environmental impact? Are you all artists? Do you have a shared faith commitment? Consider making that a focus of your intentional community.

3. Create a list of shared values and methods for interacting that build community rather than break it down. Some examples are: Agree together to look out for each other and go beyond small-talk interactions. Have a house ethic to offer help and ask for it. When conflict arises be direct and use conflict resolution rather than adversarial methods.

4. Agree to have dinner together once or twice a week. Take time at every meal to have each person share a high point and a low point since the last time you gathered. It may feel a little artificial at first, but it ensures that even the quieter people get a chance to be heard.

If intentional community is something that's not achievable right now, but you're beginning to realize it might be something you want in your living situation, start working toward that goal. Think about when your lease is up and work backward from there to find some folks you can create a community with.

. . . .

NOW DO THIS: Maybe you need to start doing something fun once a month with your roommates or start cooking together one night a week. Maybe you need a plant. Perhaps you could start a new cleaning routine. Think of three things you could do or change to make where you're living now homier, more welcoming, or just more enjoyable. Choose one of the three things to start on and then take action!

YOU ACTUALLY NEED TO KNOW: Whether you're living with others or on your own, set aside at least a little time every week or month to pay attention to your living space. Spend time and energy toward making it a place you want to be.

CHAPTER 6

MMMMM, DELISH!

(But Also Affordable, Attainable,
and Healthy-ish)

TWENTYSOMETHING TIP: Learning to plan, shop for, and prepare the foods you love to eat can be one of the biggest challenges of being on your own. Eating healthy and delicious food can make a big difference in how you feel physically and emotionally. Crank up your kitchen knowledge just a little bit and you'll be surprised at how much better you're eating—and feeling!

Do you love food? Do you love to cook? Do you love to grocery shop? If the answer to all three questions is a resounding "Yes!" then you can just skip this chapter (but you'll probably read it anyway because you enjoy all things food related). If you answered no to one or two of those questions, but especially if you answered no to all three, read on and we'll see if we can make some of these culinary conundrums a little more palatable for you. Being on your own for the first time can reveal the gaps in your adult-world skills and knowledge. If you learned how to cook, shop, and plan meals growing up, you might be wondering what the big deal is. If you didn't, kitchen issues may have you feeling a little lost. But, like any other skill set, the more you learn and practice those skills, the better you'll get.

Learn to Cook

If you find that you're living on fast food, takeout, and microwave meals, you're probably not going to change that habit completely overnight. What you can do is set a goal to cook at home one or two more nights a week than you are right now. You'll save money, and you may be surprised at how much homier your place starts to feel once you're cooking and eating there on a regular basis. Even if your eating habits aren't terrible, you may be starting to realize you could be eating better than you are. One of the nice things about learning to cook or improving your kitchen skills is that there are resources all around you. Books, websites, apps, and videos, all designed to help you cook and eat better, abound. Often the best resource of all is a friend or family member who can show you the basics plus one or two fancy tricks.

Everyone should know a few simple skills so they can feed themselves. They should also have a few extra bits of culinary knowledge so they can function socially. Making scrambled eggs can go a long way at home, but you should also know how to cook a casserole to bring to an office potluck, how to make a side dish to bring to dinner at someone else's home, and how to make something sweet to give as a gift or to cheer up a friend. And yes, you could purchase any of those things instead of making them yourself, but usually at double or triple the cost and without the personal touch and bragging rights of homemade.

If you're brand-new to cooking, choose a few basic skills and practice them. The more times you cook the better you'll get at things like sautéing vegetables, making a basic stovetop chicken dish, or even just baking brownies from a box. Getting accustomed to your tools and kitchen appliances as well as the textures, flavors, and timing of preparing different foods will serve you well. There are sure to be some disasters, but don't let them discourage you. Once you get good at a few of these skills, you'll find that you can use them without having to pay so much attention the whole time. You'll also find that the learning tends to carry over into cooking new things.

Practice these skills or feel smug if you already know how to do these things.

Beginner cooking skills checklist:

— cook pasta
— scramble eggs or make an omelet
— make pancakes or grilled cheese
— cook hamburgers in a pan, or panfry chicken, fish, or tofu
— brown ground beef
— make boxed baked goods—brownies, cakes, muffins
— cook rice
— chop and sauté vegetables

If you've already got some skills, then go for the bigger challenge. Keep your comfort foods—you know, the ones you make when you miss home or that you love so much you'll scrape the last bit out of the pan and lick the spoon. But add a few new dishes to your repertoire. Do you know how to make a fancy dessert or an impressive hors d'oeuvre? Got a solid chili recipe? Can you cook at least two dishes from another culture? How many different meals can you make from one pot of rice? Can you sharpen a knife? What sauces are you skilled at? How are you at separating eggs or making a meringue? Even just adding one or two of these extra kitchen skills to your bag of tricks can build your confidence and help you enjoy cooking rather than feeling burdened by it.

Spice It Up!

Seasoning food can make a big difference, especially if money is tight. Spices, sauces, and herbs can dress up simple inexpensive foods. The seasonings you use can introduce new and exciting flavors or evoke a sense of home and comfort. If you're saving money on food by buying family-sized packs or eating a lot of the same thing over and over, you can use different spices to add variety. Some seasonings can get pricey, but a lot of the basics can be had inexpensively. Don't know where to start? Ask your family about their most frequently used spices and get a few of your favorite recipes from home. Peruse recipes that look good to you and make lists of the seasonings they call for. You don't have to have all of them to begin cooking. A few basics will do but will vary depending on your tastes and your cultural influences.

To save money on spices, see if your local discount store carries them. If you have access to a farmer's market or international market, you might find affordable spices there. Avoid purchasing them in large quantities until you know how quickly you'll go through them. Some seasonings will go bad, get stale, or just lose their flavor before you get all the way through a big container. Another trick if you're overwhelmed by all the options is to choose a few spice mixes to try. The ratios are already worked out, they come in reasonably sized containers, and you'll always know that the spices go well together. There are many options but a few blends to try are: adobo, herbs de provence, Greek seasoning, za'atar, curry powder, Old Bay, ras el hanout, or Tony Chachere's (or other Creole or Cajun blends).

TWENTYSOMETHING TALK

The use of spices is important. If you can only afford salad or chicken, adding good spices can make a load of difference. —Sarah

When I was first learning to cook and was in an apartment with very little storage, I made so many dinners using the McCormick Complete Meal seasoning starters. Like premade taco seasoning or beef stroganoff. They have a million varieties and all come with recipes on the back. —Betsy

If you're good at growing things and you have a sunny windowsill, consider growing a few of your own fresh herbs. The flavors are even better, and they're pretty easy to grow. Good grow-your-own candidates are: basil, oregano, cilantro, and rosemary. You can use fresh or powdered garlic, onion, ginger, and thyme. And definitely try some of these basics: cinnamon, cumin, chili powder, curry, and paprika.

Make a Plan

Meal planning does not have to be complicated or time consuming but will save you a lot of stressful hungry moments staring into the fridge and wondering what the heck you're going to make with one egg, that half bag of dried-up carrots, and a can of beer. Planning can be as simple as looking at the week ahead and deciding which days you'll have the time and energy to cook and which days it makes sense to eat leftovers or eat out. Avoid making big cooking plans for longer, busier days. Think about what you'll want to eat on your "cooking days." Look at a few recipes and take note of what you've already got in the cupboard, including any seasonings you might need. Add anything you don't already have to your shopping list. Keep a running list for groceries on your phone or the front of your fridge. There are apps that can help you do all these things—meal calendars, recipes, shopping lists. If they work for you, great—just don't get bogged down in complicated planning. If you're new to meal planning, keep it super simple in the beginning and stick with what you know how to make. The more you plan your meals ahead the better you'll get at it and (eventually) the more sophisticated you can get with your plans.

TWENTYSOMETHING TALK

Meal planning is *so* helpful for keeping yourself on a budget. Try to find recipes that utilize similar ingredients so you can mix it up but not spend a ton of money buying many different ingredients. For example, chicken, veggies and rice, but maybe choose a different marinade or seasoning to keep the flavor profiles different. You can also usually cook these things all together to save time instead of making three different things back-to-back. —Jamie

Don't forget to think about lunch. Some of the meals you make at home will be great to take to work for lunch. Some foods don't travel well or are just too stinky for the office microwave. Make sure your shopping list includes at least some packable lunch foods. If you plan for it, then you can avoid the lunchtime hungry-panic-buy. That will also allow you to splurge on eating out for lunch once in a while when it's part of the plan!

TWENTYSOMETHING TALK

I bring the weirdest things to work for lunch. Sometimes it's two granola bars and an apple, sometimes it's an old yogurt container filled with last night's leftovers, sometimes it's a can of chili and a bowl—no shame! —Lilly

Meal Prepping

You can save time, money, and busy-day frustration by cooking ahead. If you don't work weekends or you have a day off, shop and cook on those days. It's one of the kindest things you can do for your future self. Cook basics in batches, then divide them up; eat one portion now, put one in the fridge for later in the week, and put one in the freezer.

TWENTYSOMETHING TALK

A lot of people don't like this option because they get bored with the food, but I make enough food to last me the entire week. I make it all Sunday and don't have to cook the rest of the week. But like I said, I eat the same meal for dinner the entire week. —Haddie

---

If you know you'd like to eat better but you're worried about how much that might cost, try some of these cost-cutting tips:

1. Check your perishables. Use up any food that can spoil first. Be in the habit of checking dates on your produce, meat, and dairy.

2. Use beans and eggs as a source of protein in some meals instead of meat.

3. Use frozen vegetables instead of fresh. They're often cheaper and you'll throw out less food because of spoiling.

4. Buy in bulk (sometimes). Everything from meat to yogurt comes in big packs. They're usually less money per pound. Be sure to only buy things you can freeze or use up before they go bad.

5. Have a list and stick to it. Avoid impulse buying. Never shop when you're hungry—your stomach will override your brain every time.

6. Buy store brands and generics instead of name-brand products. You'll get comparable quality at a fraction of the cost.

7. Avoid prepared foods. These are an expensive way to get yourself fed. The occasional splurge on a packaged dinner or supermarket sub is fine as long as it's part of your budgeted plan.

8. Purchase the right containers and supplies to store leftovers and meals you've prepped. If you store your leftovers well and safely, what was a one-shot meal can also be lunch the next day, dinner again two days later, or a nice surprise from the freezer on a night you're desperately hungry but too tired to cook.

9. Replace canned soda/Gatorade/premade beverages with stuff you make yourself. You can use your own sugar or sweetener (and a lot less of it) and save a bunch of money.

Food Safety

Keeping yourself and the people you're feeding safe from the germs that can make you sick can seem a little intimidating. It's mostly about paying attention and establishing good habits. The Centers for Disease Control and Prevention recommend four simple steps to protect against food poisoning:

1. **Clean.** Wash your hands, surfaces, and utensils with hot soapy water; rinse fresh fruits and vegetables under running water.
2. **Separate.** Don't cross-contaminate; keep raw meat, poultry, seafood, and eggs away from other foods; use separate utensils and cutting boards.
3. **Cook.** Use a meat thermometer and check a temperature chart (https://www.foodsafety.gov has a good one) to be sure you've cooked out any germs that could make you sick.
4. **Chill.** Most foods should be refrigerated within two hours and last no longer than three to four days in the refrigerator; thaw frozen foods safely (not on the counter).[1]

TWENTYSOMETHING TALK

When I first moved out my biggest struggle was probably food. I'd done laundry and dishes while living at home (although I did have a tendency to let both of those things accumulate prior to washing them), so that was familiar enough. What I hadn't done much of was cooking. In that vein, what I was most grateful for was my first slow cooker. They're dead simple to use, and you can make enough food for a week with very little effort. A five-quart one is about twenty dollars, and, in my experience, they last forever. —Paul

Kitchen Essentials

If you don't actually have a kitchen: You can emulate one with a few key appliances. An electric frying pan, a toaster oven, and a small microwave can take you a long way. Consider a slow cooker or Instant Pot too.

If you do have a kitchen but limited space: Avoid extra appliances and equipment. Choose your tools wisely, and know that, if space is limited, you can really do more with less. Preserve counter space by avoiding anything that needs to be "out" all the time. If there's no place to store a toaster, a stand mixer, a blender, or anything else that might normally take up valuable countertop real estate, get creative about where you might keep them (top of the hall closet, under your bed, along the stairs) or do without them. If you're a coffee drinker with little or no counter space, consider switching to a French press.

If you're fortunate enough to have adequate kitchen space: You may still want to be selective about how you equip it. Between space considerations and the expense of equipping your kitchen, it's worth being choosey. Start with basics and add slowly so you don't overwhelm your space or your budget.

Must-have supplies, utensils, and appliances:

- pot large enough for cooking pasta/rice
- nonstick skillet
- cutting board
- two good sharp knives: a chef's knife and a paring knife
- hand mixer

- can opener
- vegetable peeler
- set of measuring cups and spoons
- wire whisk
- dish towels
- pot holders
- baking sheet
- wooden spoons
- silicon spatula
- mixing bowls
- colander
- glass casserole dish

Extras to consider: An iron skillet, muffin pan, loaf pan, pie plate, and/or set of small round cake pans—but if you only bake once or twice a year, consider foil pans to save the storage space.

Not vital but fans swear by them: Garlic press, food processer, panini press/electric grill, Crock-Pot, or Instant Pot.

NOW DO THIS: What's your biggest struggle when it comes to food? Is it shopping, meal prep, eating healthily, finding food you love? Type the problem into your search bar. Read at least three articles on the problem and choose two positive steps to take.

YOU ACTUALLY NEED TO KNOW: Food is such a big part of our lives. Learning to eat well but inexpensively is a great skill to cultivate. Paying attention to what and why you're eating will help you be both healthy and happy.

CHAPTER 7

MY STUFF, MY SELF

Sorting Out Essentials from Excess

TWENTYSOMETHING TIP: Your twenties are a great time to look around at your life and figure out what you want to carry with you into the future and what you're ready to leave behind.

Having limited space and a sometimes-
nomadic habit as a twentysomething can be a blessing and a curse. It can force some heartrending decisions about letting go of things you'd rather hang on to and might even be able to use at some point in the future. But it also helps you prioritize what you really value and what you actually need. It helps you shed the excess stuff that can become clutter. Not only that, it may even help you develop the difficult-to-acquire discipline of saying no to allowing the extra stuff into your life in the first place.

Raised to Consume

There are tons of good reasons to lighten your load possessions-wise and to be discriminating about future purchases. Our consumer economy has trained us to buy, buy, buy, whether we need a thing or not. In our culture we can respond to almost any feeling with a purchase. Sad? Maybe a little treat will pick up your mood. Bored? Let's go shopping. Frustrated? Distract yourself with something new. Maybe that hasn't been your experience. Count yourself lucky if someone in your life taught you to stop and think about things like: who made the thing you're about to purchase, what their working conditions might be like, or where this thing will go when you're done with it. Happily, more and more people are beginning to ask those kinds of questions. Out of concern for human rights, the impact on the environment, and our own mental health, people are also beginning to ask, "Will more stuff actually make me happier?" It turns out that, for the most part, the answer is no.

Not surprisingly, being able to provide for basic needs figures significantly into human happiness. Once those basic needs are met, though, more money and more things don't actually make a person happier.[1] Purchases that help us pursue an interest or tap into our creativity (art supplies for an artist, a new bicycle for a cycling enthusiast) can impact our happiness because they help us do something we enjoy.[2] Spending habits that help us learn new things, tend to our relationships, and have new experiences can add to feelings of happiness. Conversely, the sometimes-addictive urge for something new can be a problem. Instead of approaching a new purchase thoughtfully, an impulse buy, after the initial rush of pleasure, can sometimes lead to feelings of guilt or shame. If you are having trouble distinguishing wants from needs, visit chapter 12 and read about habits and some of the signs that let you know if your spending is starting to become a problem.

We often know, at least deep inside, the difference between something we need and something we want. Most spiritual traditions have practices to help with detaching from the things we own and cautions about the accumulation of possessions. It's one aspect of asceticism and is related to practices like fasting and giving to the poor. All of these are actions that help remind us that we are more than what we own. They help us value who we are and our connection to other people more.

Artificial Affluence

One of the challenges of first being on your own is that, in the past, you may have had more than you needed. If you were accustomed to having everything you needed provided by family, with any income you brought in yourself used for wants—eating out, entertainment, impulse buys, travel—once you're on your own you may start feeling some sense of deprivation. The affluence you experienced when you were floating along on the top of your family's income gave you an artificial sense of what you could afford. Now, even if you have everything you need, if you can't afford all the things you want, it can be a surprise. If you're going through this now, give yourself some time to adjust. Believe it or not there are serious benefits to having to stop and make choices about the way you spend your money. It's a very adult thing to do. Learning to not immediately give in to every demand or desire you feel can help you in several ways. It helps you discern between needs and wants. It helps you recognize that how happy you are doesn't have to be tied to always having the money to do whatever you want whenever you want. And it helps you get better at setting goals and meeting them if you have to prioritize and save for a special trip, concert, or splurge purchase.

Lighten the Load?

Maybe you're one of those lucky few who doesn't accumulate too many possessions as you move through life. If you're like most people, though, you probably have the tendency to pick up more stuff as you go along. Here are some more reasons for keeping possessions to a minimum:

1. It reduces the amount of time you spend taking care of your stuff—storing, cleaning, sorting, protecting.
2. It actually costs money to keep excess around; you don't necessarily notice it, but you (or whomever is storing your stuff) can reduce that cost or free that space by hanging on to less.
3. Every time you move, the accumulated stuff must be purged or packed. The more stuff you have, the more work this will be.
4. There's a mental load that goes along with having too much stuff. There can be shame and embarrassment connected to accumulated possessions as well as anxiety connected to what to do about it.

Sorting Through Your Stuff

If you're living with family now and are able to access your stuff, consider trying to go through a box a week or sort through your accumulated stuff a little at a time. When the day comes to go off on your own, you'll have already chosen what to keep and gotten rid of the excess. Sometimes that has to happen in a flurry, and it can be hard to sift through everything at once. Here are a few organizing tricks that might help with either process:

1. If you won't use it or wear it or play it or read it again, do your absolute best to pass it on to someone who will. (If it doesn't fit now, do yourself the kindness of letting it go.)
2. If it's broken and you love it, get it fixed. If it's broken and you don't love it or it's outdated or it's been broken for more than a year, recycle or toss as appropriate.
3. If you're having a hard time parting with something, take a picture of it and see if that will do the trick as a keepsake.
4. Allow yourself a box or two of mementos. Use a sturdy moisture-proof container that will protect your keep-sakes. Choose a few important items and store them well. This can free you to get rid of the less important clutter.
5. If you're finding that you can't bear to part with anything at all, find a buddy. A friend who is kind but firm can help you sort through the excess and coach you through letting the unnecessary things go.
6. Label each "keep" box you pack up with a list of its contents. That way you won't have to go through everything to find one thing.

TWENTYSOMETHING TALK

I try not to buy things, and if I want to get rid of something, I try to find a way to give it to a friend or family or donate it or recycle it. Being eco-friendly is really important to me, so I try to reduce/reuse/recycle as much as possible. —Brandon

When we suddenly upgraded a bunch of kitchen stuff when we got married, we asked if our friends needed anything first. (Moving is a great way to determine what you don't need sometimes!) Before donating to Goodwill or the Salvation Army, look for nonprofits that could use what you are retiring (shelters, churches, community kitchens). If you have older nonperishables, bring them to a food pantry! —Morgan

---

8 Ways to Avoid Buying New

There are, of course, some things you'll want or need to buy new, but there's a lot you can get free and cheap through the following means:

1. **Ask friends and family if they have anything they're looking to get rid of.** People are often seeking to lighten their own load. You can always let them know what it is you're looking for and that you're looking for free or cheap.

2. **Swap your stuff with friends.** Have a party and ask friends to bring their still-usable castoffs, the things they would donate anyway. You can host one for clothes and accessories (jewelry, shoes, purses), household items (small appliances, lamps, pictures, linens), kitchen items, books, art supplies, or almost anything that people might want or need.

3. **Barter.** Let people know what you have to trade or teach and let them know what you need.

4. **Find things online for free.** Search the Freecycle Network, the Craigslist "free stuff" section, Buy Nothing

Project groups on Facebook, and depending on where you live, other social media too.

5. **Buy things secondhand online.** Browse sites like Letgo, ThredUp, eBay, Facebook Marketplace, and Nextdoor for gently worn/used items.

6. **Shop at IRL secondhand stores.** Swing by local consignment shops, thrift stores, flea markets, garage sales, and community rummage sales in search of affordable items and hidden gems.

7. **Take advantage of move-out day.** In college towns move-out season is a good time to look locally online and to swing by the dorms and see what people are leaving by the dumpster.

8. **Shop other people's returns.** For things that are harder to find used and reliable (like certain electronics), consider open-box and refurbished purchases from trustworthy vendors.

TWENTYSOMETHING TALK

I love secondhand shopping! Aside from saving money, I enjoy the hunt of looking for things you need. You also find some super cool pieces. —Haddie

For some big purchases I will look into open-box or used options first (game consoles, cell phone)—things that you can get specifics on if the item works as well as you need it to before purchasing. Whether it's for myself or a gift for someone, I almost always wait to make a nonessential purchase until it's on sale. If a website has a referral program, ask for referral codes! —Morgan

---

> **NOW DO THIS:** Make a list of the things you still need. Prioritize based on urgency. Mark the things you may be able to buy secondhand.
>
> **YOU ACTUALLY NEED TO KNOW:** Make the assessment and answer the questions for yourself: What's extra, and what do I still need? Your closets, your budget, and your future self will all be better for it.

CHAPTER 8

BUDGETING FOR BEGINNERS

Making the Most of Your Money

TWENTYSOMETHING TIP: Create a budget, pay down your debt, and learn how to get a handle on credit. Do these things, then reap the rewards: less worry and knowing what you can spend.

Even if you have a full-time job at a decent wage and are not a habitual overspender, making ends meet can be one of the hardest things about being in your twenties. If you've been covering your own expenses for a while, it may not seem like a big deal anymore. But if you're new to handling all your own financial responsibilities, it can take a bit of practice to figure out how to avoid coming up short at the end of the month. If you're currently living somewhere affordable and have money coming in, then stay put for a hot minute while you figure out your finances and save up an emergency fund. You may never need it, but if you do, you may need it badly. Are you already in the thick of things and have more money going out than coming in? Don't panic, but do budget. Find a budgeting system that works for you, and once you do, stick to it like jam on a sandwich.

Make a Plan

There's an awful lot of advice available about getting a handle on your money. The trick is finding what works for you. Being realistic about how much you'll have coming in, especially if you have income that fluctuates from month to month or week to week, is a vital first step. Next, an honest look at how you tend to spend your money will help. Finally, making a plan that has more money coming in than going out each month will get you moving in the right direction. Sounds simple, right? Keep in mind that as you make that plan, life keeps happening. Unexpected expenses arise. Cars break down. A utility bill is higher than expected. You don't make as much this month as you planned to. You get the chance to go on a trip or see a show you didn't budget for. So you need a plan, but the plan needs some flexibility. These tips and tricks can help you build a good, flexible plan:

1. **Get thee an app.** If you do most of your banking online, find an app or software program you like to help you manage your money. Check out a few of them to find the best fit for you. Mint (free) and You Need a Budget (has a fee) are both good.

2. **Track your spending.** At least for the first few months, write down (or use your app to track) where every dollar goes. You have to know where your money has been going if you want to make informed choices about where it should be going.

3. **Identify your wants, needs, and savings goals.** Experts will give you all kinds of rules about what portion of your income you should be devoting to your essential living expenses versus your "wants" versus your savings/investments. The 50/20/30 rule and the 70/20/10 rule are some of the most popular formulas to

help you determine how to distribute your income across these three categories. If your bottom-line necessities eat up 85 percent of your income, it's going to be tight. The two things everybody seems to agree on: save at least 10 percent of what you're earning, and spend no more than 30 percent on housing.

4. **Expect the unexpected.** Expenses will pop up here and there: you may need to replace a phone or computer that fritzes out or attend a wedding, shower, or party you didn't plan on in advance. Build some of those costs into your budget. If nothing bad happens, you have a nice little bonus. If it does, you'll be ready.

5. **Plan for the expensive months all year long.** Even though you're making a *monthly* budget, some expenses occur annually or semiannually. You know these are coming up, so calculate your total annual expenses, divide by twelve, and include this in your monthly budget.

When you start handling your own finances, you may reassess the ways you've spent money in the past. If you never worried before about running out of money or having enough to do the things you want to do, that's nice. This new financially independent world may be a bracing experience. If you grew up with less, you actually may have a bit of an advantage over your well-to-do peers here in that you probably know how to cut corners and sort through the needs vs. wants questions more easily. Either way, do not get discouraged. There are so many ways to spend less and save more. Let's look at a few of them.

Cutting Expenses

The basic needs—food, shelter, and clothing—are needs, and there's no getting around that. With a little bit of know-how, though, you can save fistfuls of money in each of these categories. Let's start with food. Pay attention to what you're buying and where you're buying it. You'll pay more at a convenience store than at the grocery store, which is more expensive than the wholesale place, which may cost more than the farmers' market. You can save money on groceries by buying in bulk, using coupons, shopping the sales, buying store brands instead of brand-name products. Learn some new skills and sharpen others—meal planning, cooking, using leftovers, and freezing extras. Seek out inexpensive proteins: beans, eggs, peanut butter, tuna fish, cheese, to name a few. Making your own snacks, drinks, dressings and sauces, dips, and mixes (cake, brownie, biscuit, pancake) can save a bunch. Save money eating out by going out for breakfast or lunch. They're cheaper than dinner. The markup on alcohol is huge, so eat out but don't drink out. (Or drink less when you're out.) Knock down your restaurant check by ten to forty dollars by having appetizers or dessert (or both) at home. For more food-savings tips, revisit chapter 6.

Obviously if you can live with family for free or cheap without driving each other crazy, it's a great way to sock away money until you can get to your dream living situation. If that's not possible, there are lots of other ways to save on shelter costs. Live one neighborhood out from where you'd like to be; enjoy the nearness of the trendy places without the extra expense. Different units in the same complex may rent for less because of the view (or lack of one). If you're in a position to, consider buying, then renting out rooms to friends or strangers. Get the tax advantages of owning plus the financial benefits of sharing with housemates. Revisit chapter 3 for more tips on apartment savings.

The strain on your wallet from clothing can be almost nothing or it can break your budget, depending on what you do for work and how often you have to be dressed all the way up. You can save by shopping the sales, buying secondhand (online or consignment/thrift shops), limiting "trend spending," and relying more on classic pieces that will last multiple seasons. If you have friends who are similarly sized and shaped as you, clothing swaps or sharing your closets can be good money-saving solutions.

TWENTYSOMETHING TALK

I'm terrible at getting things I want. If you don't need it to live (food, shelter, water, some transportation), then you don't need it. —Ryan

After finally getting a regular paying job, it was very tempting to get stuff that I had been waiting to get. Make sure to pace yourself, give yourself saving goals, set hard limits (takeout once a week, for example). —Morgan

Entertainment and Exercise

Life is more than work, and the health benefits, physical and mental, of recreation cannot be overstated. Having fun and staying fit can get expensive, but there are unexpected ways to save money and ease the impact on your budget. Review your subscriptions—video, music, and gaming. It's easy to burn a lot of your budget on services you don't use or don't use much. If it feels too wrenching to get rid of them completely, try taking a break from the ones you use the least. See if you miss them. If you decide you can't afford them at all, remember your public library also loans music, audiobooks, e-books, movies, video games, and e-readers. Instead of paying a monthly fee to listen to music on your commute, try switching to a podcast or an audiobook.

A gym membership can be expensive, and there are lots of ways to get your workouts in without one. Look online for fitness resources and channels. If you run, walk, hike, or bike, look to local organizations for recommendations on the best trails. That said, a membership may be an expense you decide is worth it, so look for discounts and deals. If you can't justify the expense of a membership or if you need the accountability of a group, look for less expensive community classes and clubs. Watch out for equipment costs with any activity and consider taking a break from activities that have big price tags.

If expensive travel, big-ticket concerts or sports, or other pricey forms of play have been part of your past, especially if you haven't had to foot that bill, not being able to afford these things now can be a big disappointment. Be realistic about what you can swing. Decide which events are worth what you'll have to sacrifice or how much overtime you'll have to put in. If these have been big memory makers for you and your group of friends, let them know you're trying to save money and you might like to try some less expensive options. You're probably not the only one in your group feeling the pinch of being twentysomething.

Transportation

If you live in a city with decent public transportation or where walking or biking is an option, you can free up a good deal of the income that might have been spent on a vehicle. Public transportation can take a little more planning, as can getting to work under your own steam (walking or biking)—especially when the weather is anything other than sunny and mild—but the savings can make the inconvenience well worth it.

Depending on where you're living and working, you may or may not have to rely on owning a car—or at least having access to the use of one. It's worth questioning that requirement if you've assumed you have to have a car and it has to be your own. If you're living with family and willing to do a little advance planning each week about who needs to get where when, you can save quite a bit of money by sharing. If you decide you have to have one, a used car will be less expensive to buy and insure. Your most expensive option is to buy your own new car. Experts say that if you do have to finance a vehicle, use the 20/4/10 rule: Make a down payment equal to 20 percent of the total price, limit the life of the loan to four years, and spend no more than 10 percent of your gross income on your monthly payments.

Loaning Money

Whether or not to lend money to a friend in need can be a hard decision, but the rule is this: if you can't afford to lose it, you can't afford to loan it. Never answer on the spot. Anytime anyone asks you for money, say you have to check your budget/bank balance/cash on hand/whatever; don't ever be pressured into saying yes immediately. Even if you know you *could* say yes, give yourself some time to think it over first. If you do say yes, do not count on getting that money back. You can expect it, hope for it, dream of it—that's fine—but do not make it part of your budgeting or financial plan.

Pay Your Bills On Time, Every Time

If you are earning enough money to pay your bills, paying them on time is the single best thing you can do for your finances. With very few exceptions, nearly everything can be paid online. Most companies are happy to set you up with automatic billing; for those that don't offer it, many banks will set up electronic payments for you. Either way, your payment will be deducted from your bank account whenever it is due and delivered to your payee using the magical powers of the internet.

Before you set up automated payments, set up a safety net for yourself in the form of overdraft protection on your checking account. One bounced check or payment and the accompanying fees can quickly turn into a financial disaster as one payment after another hits an overdrawn account. If your balance goes negative, you can be hit with a fee of around thirty-five dollars for each transaction. In order to stop racking up fees, you first have to pay all those fees that have already been charged. As you might imagine, it gets ugly and expensive really fast—especially if lack of money was the reason you went negative in the first place. (Tip: Always go to the bank in person and ask them if they will reverse any of the charges. They'll usually knock off one or two if you have a good history with them.)

Keep all your payment dates on your calendar. If you're not using autopay, that will be your reminder, and if you are, it will remind you that your current bank balance doesn't tell you the whole story about how much money you actually have.

Savings

How much is enough when it comes to savings? Experts say that it's a good idea to keep six months' worth of expenses in a savings account, in case of unexpected job loss, a serious health event, a global pandemic, etc. So if your monthly expenses total $2,000, then you should have $12,000 in savings. That may or may not be a realistic goal for you. If those figures did not make you laugh, then that's the advice you should follow. If they did make you laugh, see if you can at least squirrel away enough to live on for an extra month or two.

Different strategies work for different people when it comes to saving. Contributing to your savings should be part of your monthly budget. One of the easiest ways to ensure this happens every month is direct deposit or auto transfers. Have part of your pay go into your checking account and automatically route a certain portion of it into one or more different accounts for savings. The rationale here is that if you don't have it, you can't spend it (frivolously). People say that the portion of their earnings they never see, they never miss. Unless you are carrying a significant amount of high-interest debt, this is a great way to hang onto money you don't want to mindlessly fritter away.

TWENTYSOMETHING TALK

Save, save, save. Set up a recurring transfer to a savings account every paycheck. Getting a raise is a *great* opportunity to do this. Take the amount of your raise and make that your recurring deposit to savings since you're already used to living on your current salary.
—Jamie

Debt and Credit

We've talked a lot about what to do with money that you do have. But what if you're broke? What if you have no money, or worse than that, less than no money (also known as debt).

If you've been to college at all, chances are you've got student loans. Even if you had a college fund that your parents regularly contributed to when you were growing up, the cost of college has increased by at least 25 percent (some sources say up to 55 percent) just in the past ten years, so chances are your fund was not enough to cover four or more years of school.

College is not the only place to accumulate debt. Credit cards, medical bills, and car loans, just to name a few, can easily spiral out of control through no fault of your own—job loss, the end of a relationship, an abrupt change in living situation, a depressive episode, a family crisis, etc. And maybe you made some rookie mistakes that contributed to your less-than-stellar financial situation. Give yourself a break. Twenty-first-century life is complicated and difficult, and it's your first time!

Your Credit Score

Your credit score is a number used by your prospective lenders and landlords to determine if you are a decent credit risk—someone who is likely to make payments on time. Based on this number, lenders will determine not only whether to loan you money but also how much they're going to charge you for it; the better your credit score, the lower your interest rate.

Your lenders (a credit card company, the bank that holds your auto loan, etc.) will report your payment behavior to one or more major credit reporting agencies. They calculate the information and give you a score. Anything over 800 is considered excellent, around 700 is good, and under 580 is considered poor. The two most important factors that affect your credit score are your payment history and credit utilization.

Payment history: Just like it sounds, this is the history of all the payments you've made, including whether or not they were on time. Be aware that not just credit cards and loans but in some cases utilities, your cell phone, medical bills, and the like may also be reported.

Credit utilization: This refers to how much of your available credit you're using (it only includes revolving credit, not installment credit—see "credit mix" below), and it should be not too much, not too little, but just right. You want to use less than 30 percent of your available credit—30 percent on each individual account and 30 percent in total. So if you've got two credit cards, each with a $1,000 limit, you should have a balance of under $300 on each of them. If you've got $600 on one (60 percent credit utilization on this account) and $0 on the other (0 percent on the second account but still 30 percent overall), that's worse for your credit score (see table below). Of course, if one account has a lower interest rate, you will save money by keeping the whole balance on that card. You'll have to decide which is more important in the short term; in the long term the best plan is to pay it all off as soon as you can.

First Account	Second Account	Total
$300 balance on $1,000 limit = **30 percent**	$300 balance on $1,000 limit = **30 percent**	$600 balance of $2,000 limit = **30 percent**
$600 balance on $1,000 limit = **60 percent**	$0 balance on $1,000 limit = **0 percent**	$600 balance of $2,000 limit = **30 percent**

At the same time, you do want to use your credit cards at least once in a while. If you never use an account at all, the credit card company may close it. While it's fine for you to close out a card, if the credit card company does it, your score will take a hit. There are four other factors that can impact your credit score less dramatically but are worth knowing if you're trying to improve it:

1. **Length of credit history.** The longer your credit history the better. For this reason you may want to avoid closing an older credit card, especially if it doesn't have an annual fee.

2. **Credit mix.** There are two main types of credit. Installment credit refers to loans in which you borrow a set amount and pay it back in scheduled (usually monthly) installments. Revolving credit refers to an account (credit card or store card) that allows you to spend up to a certain limit and pay it back as quickly or slowly as you like, provided that you make a minimum payment each month.

Having both types will help your credit score by demonstrating that you can handle them both responsibly.

3. **Too many credit checks.** When a lender reviews your credit report to help decide whether or not to approve your application, it's often referred to as "running a credit check," but technically it's called a hard inquiry (this is different from you checking your own report). Multiple hard inquiries within a short time can hurt your credit score, so if you're applying for more than one or two accounts, or if you're applying for a loan at several different banks, try to space them out at least six months.

4. **New credit.** Similarly, if you have opened more than one new account recently, you can expect your score to take a hit.

To find out your credit score, you can use an app like Credit Karma or, if you already have a credit card, check your statement or your online account—many companies will provide you with it free of charge.

TWENTYSOMETHING TALK

Overspending is *so* hard! All those credit card companies want to give you credit cards and they up your spending limits and you see all this "money" you have. Use credit only when you need it. Sure you need to use credit to build credit, but make sure you're only spending what you can pay off at the end of the month to avoid interest. It compounds, so it can be hard to catch up later. —Jamie

---

Your Credit Report

If your score is currently less than stellar, check your credit report. You can do this for free once per year at the official website, AnnualCreditReport.com. Your credit report includes that payment history we talked about and all the other information that your credit score is based on, but it does not include your numerical score. If you find an error on your credit report, you should write to the information provider (for instance, your phone company) and the credit reporting agency where you got the report. Keep a copy of all your correspondence. They are legally required to investigate your claim. You may be the victim of fraud or the victim of a clerical or computer error. You can get more information (and nobody trying to sell you anything) from the government website: https://www.usa.gov/credit-reports.

Credit Cards

Credit cards can build your credit, but they also have the potential to ruin it. You can save yourself a lot of future troubles by doing two things. First, recognize your credit card as a tool to build a positive credit history. Second, realize the dangers of using it to spend money that you don't have. Your credit card issuer makes money off of you. They are professionals at this, and your credit card company is never going to willingly take any action that is to their own detriment.

Here are the steps for using a credit card to your advantage:

1. Find one with a low interest rate, no annual fee, and a great rewards program.
2. Use it only for purchases you already have enough money to cover or for absolute emergencies.
3. Pay off the entire balance in full every single month.
4. Never get a cash advance.

One tiny misstep here can plunge you into a debt spiral. Potential pitfalls include late fees, over-limit fees, only paying your monthly minimum (it can take over thirty years to pay off even a small balance this way, and the finance charges can easily be four or five times as much as you ever charged to your card in the first place). Thanks to consumer protection laws, credit card companies are now required to include two numbers on your monthly statement. The first is how long it will take you to pay off your current balance if you only make the minimum payments, and the second is how much you would need to pay each month in order to pay off the whole balance in three years.

Getting Out of Debt

Debt can spin out of control in no time, or it can be a manageable but gloomy cloud hanging over your head. Either way, debt feels good to get rid of. Fortunately, solutions and strategies do exist.

Here are some ways to work your way up and out, and get on top of your finances:

1. **Pay it down.** In order to avoid accumulating more debt and worse credit in the form of late fees and other charges, keep making at least the minimum payments on every account, each month, on time. Mathematically it makes sense to pay off the account with the highest interest rate first (typically credit cards are highest and student loans are lowest). This way you end up paying less interest and therefore less money overall.

2. **Transfer your balances.** If your credit is not terrible but the debt load you're carrying (or your interest rate) is higher than you'd like, you may qualify to open a new credit card account with a lower rate and transfer one or more balances to it. Balance transfers often carry a 0 percent interest rate, at least on a temporary basis. You can also use this new account to make payments on other accounts—an auto loan, for instance—in effect lowering your interest rate on that debt. This will both give you some breathing room in the short term and also save you money in the long run.

3. **Take out a debt consolidation loan.** This is similar to transferring all your balances to one credit account, but instead of using revolving credit, it uses installment credit (see "Your Credit Score"). In this case you would apply to a bank or credit union for a personal loan in the total amount of the debts you want to consolidate. You might include all your credit card debts and medical bills, but not your

student loans, for instance. If you are approved for the loan, the money is then used to pay off those creditors in full, and you will in turn pay one easy installment to your new lender every month until the loan is repaid.

4. **Negotiate.** Creditors don't advertise this, but you can often get them to lower your payment or interest rate just by asking. If you're having a hard time making your payments, call them up. They are in the business of making money, so you might think they'd be unwilling to cut you a deal, but they also know that if you end up in bankruptcy, they risk getting nothing.

5. **Seek credit counseling.** Nonprofit credit counseling agencies exist to help people with their finances. (The Federal Trade Commission has guidelines available on their website to help you choose a reputable organization.)

6. **File bankruptcy.** Bankruptcy is the end of the line. Approach with caution, but don't rule it out altogether. If you already have bad credit and you don't think you can pay your debt off within the next seven years, talk to a credit counselor or a lawyer (most offer a free initial consultation). In many cases you can keep your home and your car and begin rebuilding good credit right away.

Creditors and Collections

Debt collection generally goes through three stages. The first stage is when you borrow money with an agreement about how and when to pay it back (like a loan or credit card) or obtain a service (like electricity) based on an agreement to pay for it in a certain time frame. Your account begins "in good standing" or "up to date," meaning that you are fulfilling your end of the agreement. The second stage is "delinquency," or when you have not been paying your accounts as agreed but your original creditors (utility company, credit card issuer, hospital, etc.) are still attempting to collect the payment. Once they have given up on doing this themselves, they may sell your debt to a collection agency, at which point your debt reaches the third and final stage, "in collections."

The Dos and Don'ts of Dealing with Debt Collectors

It's no fun being in a situation where your creditors are calling you on the phone asking about your payments, but if that's a situation you ever find yourself in, this may help:

1. **Don't answer the phone.** You are under no obligation to accept a phone call, especially not on someone else's schedule. You are under no obligation to speak with people who are being rude or unkind to you (even if you do owe them, or the company they work for, money). But . . .

2. **Do answer the phone.** Even though it's an unpleasant task, it may well be worth the pain. As a general rule

(especially if your debt is in stage two rather than stage three), they aren't calling to be mean to you, harass you, or judge you. They are calling to remind you in case you forgot to make the payment or potentially to alert you to a bank problem if you did make the payment; they may even be calling to offer you help in the form of reduced or deferred payments. At the very least, answering the phone and telling them you can only afford to send them ten dollars this month may stop them from calling you again until next month.

3. **Don't bother lying.** It doesn't do you any good to say that you're going to make a payment when you know you can't make a payment. They're just going to call you again when they don't get it. If you don't tell your creditors you're having trouble making your payments, they probably won't offer you any assistance, so just like the saying goes, honesty is the best policy.

4. **Do know your rights.** Collection agencies (who own your debt if it has reached the third stage, explained on page 139) have been known to use underhanded tactics to try to collect money. Debtors are legally protected from harassment by the 1977 Fair Debt Collection Practices Act, but debt collectors are notorious for ignoring this law. Fortunately, it's easy to find information online detailing what they're not allowed to do and how you can make them stop if you are being harassed. Try the nonprofit Debt.org to get started.

How to Do Your Taxes

You can do this. Really, you can. The IRS website has an interactive tax assistant, which will guide you through a short interview to determine whether or not you are legally required to file. Even if you don't have to file, you may be entitled to a refund, so it's worth checking. If you own your own business or have any dependents, your taxes may be a bit more complicated. Even still, for most people, filing taxes is a manageable task.

1. **Get your papers together.** Anyone who is sending you a form that you will need in order to complete your tax return (like your employer or your health insurance company) is required to do so by January 31. If you know you should have received something (like a W-2 from a previous employer, for instance) but it hasn't arrived, give them a call and track it down sooner rather than later.

2. **Understand your options for filing.** There are still paper forms, but most people find it easier to e-file. Tax software is available for purchase, but unless your taxes are especially complicated, you can find a free version that's more than adequate. The software will guide you through a series of questions and, using your answers, will digitally fill out the forms and do all your calculations for you. Another option is to hire an accountant or tax preparer to complete your return for you. It will cost you money but save you time and frustration, especially if your situation is more complex.

3. **Don't wait until Tax Day.** The filing deadline is midnight at the end of April 15 (unless it's a weekend or holiday), and your tax return has to be either postmarked or electronically filed by then (or by the end of the next business day if April 15 is a holiday) in order to be on time. If for any reason you can't meet the deadline, be sure to avoid a late-filing penalty by filing for an extension instead. Once you have everything you need, though, you can file anytime after January 1. If you think you will be receiving a refund, go ahead and get it done! The sooner you file, the sooner you get the money. If you owe money to the IRS, it is due at the same time as you file your refund, so the only reason to wait would be if you need more time to get your payment together. If you owe money and cannot pay it all at once, you can set up a payment plan on the IRS website.

4. **Save a copy.** Experts recommend keeping a copy of your tax return on file for at least three years after the filing date. There are limits on how long the IRS has to audit you under certain circumstances, but there is no limitation if they suspect fraud or if you didn't file (or if they say you didn't file, in which case you may need your copies in order to prove that you did).

TWENTYSOMETHING TALK

When I was younger, my mom taught me how to pay bills: keeping track of when they're due, how much they are, how each company prefers to be paid (many offer discounts for linked bank accounts and paperless billing), and being consistent with it are probably the best things I took away. Also, an emergency [savings] cushion is important; it keeps you from having to live on ramen for a month because you busted a tire. —Sarah

---

NOW DO THIS: Research and then take one small step to improve your credit rating.

YOU ACTUALLY NEED TO KNOW: Taking the time to develop stronger financial habits and clean up your credit can pay off in less stress, more fun, and actual money!

PART 3

REAL RELATIONSHIPS FOR REAL LIFE

CHAPTER 9

NOT A KID ANYMORE

Navigating Family Relationships as an Adult

TWENTYSOMETHING TIP: It can be hard for families to remember that the kid they've known for twenty years or more isn't a kid anymore. Carving out an adult identity within your family of origin doesn't happen overnight, but it can happen—and you can help it along.

Families are challenging and weird. The very same family can be wonderful at times and terrible at other times. If you were raised in a strong, positive, mostly supportive family, you probably already know how lucky you are. Healthy families foster independence. They are there when you need them with minimal conditions on the help they offer. Growing up in a family like that can give you a great start and continue to be an advantage throughout your life. If your circumstances were less ideal, if there was high conflict, abuse or control, or mental health or addiction issues that went untended, you may have work to do as an adult to recover from that. Doing that work (through therapy, learning, and intention) lessens the chances that you'll carry that harm with you into the rest of your life. For most of us it's a mixed bag. There were things our families did well and other things they struggled with or even just messed up completely.

It can be hard for our families to adjust to our new adult selves. They've often not seen the growth and change we've experienced as closely as our friends have. One of the best things about being an adult is that you get a new set of choices about how you relate to your family. As a kid it's unlikely you had a choice about the family you were in. You probably had little or no awareness about your role in your family, and as that awareness dawned, you may not have had much idea how to change or influence that role. As an adult you get to, and ought to, make conscious choices about what kind of relationship you want to have with the family you grew up in.

Disappearing Markers

A generation or two ago the line between adolescence and adulthood was pretty clearly marked. The signs of adulthood were obvious: the shift to financial independence, a job that paid the bills, marriage—or at least a serious relationship—and having children. In a fairly short period, nearly every one of those boundary lines has either changed completely or seen a significant shift. The dramatic increase in college debt, the rising age of marriage (and in some demographics the disappearance of it), a collapsed economy, and a changed job market have all turned those traditional markers of adulthood on their ear.

So if none of the old signs of adulthood work anymore, does that mean the boundary line is gone? Or is it just a little harder to make out? Adulthood is still marked by an increased sense of independence—of being responsible, able to make your own choices, and capable of setting limits for yourself.

According to researcher Jeffrey Jensen Arnett, who identified "emerging adulthood" as a distinct developmental stage, the five main features of this stage are:

1. **Identity explorations:** answering the question "who am I?" and trying out various life options, especially in love and work;

2. **Instability:** in love, work, and place of residence;
3. **Self-focus:** as obligations to others reach a lifespan low point;
4. **Feeling in-between:** in transition, neither adolescent nor adult; and
5. **Possibilities/optimism:** when hopes flourish and people have an unparalleled opportunity to transform their lives.[1]

As you can see from Arnett's description, and as your life experience so far has probably shown you, adulthood is not the flipping of a switch. Becoming an adult is a process that is already well underway in you. If you are still feeling a little in-between, that's to be expected. And if your family is having a tough time recognizing that you are an adult, it's not all that surprising.

Obviously whether you live with your family right now will have a huge impact on just how much it matters if they recognize you as an adult or not. (You can find more specific advice about living with your parents as an adult in chapter 4.) The wear and tear on the relationship may not be as severe or persistent if you're not sharing living space, but it will still be there and is often worth trying to improve.

You can't change another person, of course, but you can encourage your family to change their interactions with you by how you respond to them. If you're feeling frustrated about those interactions, try one or more of these approaches:

1. **Don't let them push your buttons.** The people who have known us longest often know exactly how to get

under our skin. If you find yourself getting upset during an interaction, try to keep calm, step away if you need to, but remember you can establish a new pattern simply by reacting differently than you have in the past. That knowledge can be one of the most empowering things of all.

2. **Have hard conversations.** Address problems. Rather than letting problems get worse until they reach a boiling point, let your family know that you'd like to talk about the issue. If you can, set a time when you can have an uninterrupted conversation without distractions. Some problems will take several conversations, and that's okay.

3. **Pick your battles.** Especially if you have a high-conflict family, understand that every single fight does not have to be fought. It's okay to just address the most important things or the things that are making your life the most difficult. When you do assert yourself on an issue, be as calm as you can be. Keeping a cool head can help change the way your family perceives you.

4. **Be as honest with them as you can.** If you don't give your family the chance to help you in a particular struggle, if you never tell them that what they're doing is a problem for you or that you need their support on something, you may be missing out on what could be a positive transformation for everyone involved.

5. **Have a private life.** As an adult you get to decide which parts of your life your family needs to be involved in. Your family does not have a right to complete knowledge

about and access to your entire life simply because they're related to you.

6. **Be a listener.** Show your family that you are ready to hear what they have to say and seriously consider their point(s) of view. Practicing respectful listening sets an example that you can ask them to follow.

7. **Write it down.** If you come from a family that tends to talk over each other or has a hard time hearing each other out, try putting your thoughts in writing. It can help you get all your points down and gives the other person a chance to reflect on those points before responding. Follow up with a conversation.

TWENTYSOMETHING TALK

If you can show them that you're doing great being independent, they'll eventually stop treating you like a kid. You can also say things like, "Hey I really appreciate you checking in with me every other day, but I'm grown-up now and can handle things on my own. I know I can always come to you for help when I need it." Showing them that they're still important and you can go to them when you need them helps them reign in their coddling. —Jamie

Sometimes you really need to stand your ground, and it can have consequences, but it's important to establish that you can't always be influenced, forced, or guilted into what your family's agenda is. —Morgan

How to Be Considerate

One of the things you might not have considered is how considerate you are of your family. It's easy for anyone to take their family for granted. We get back home and suddenly we revert, at least about some things, to old habits from when we were kids. There are often many little things that our parents do that we don't even notice. What are some of the things your parents still pay for? When you get together with family what's provided? What things do you use that belong to your parents? Beyond the material, parents often listen to us and want to know how we're doing. They root for us and want us to be successful and happy. We don't have to feel guilty about any of that, but we should acknowledge it.

When you're spending time with your family, notice your own behavior. Are you as considerate toward them as if you were visiting a friend? Do you bring part of the meal or help prepare or set up? Do you help clean up after? Are you polite? Do you say please and thank you? You shouldn't feel like you have to behave like a stranger or guest, but showing appreciation for the things you may not have noticed or acknowledged before can create a new dynamic in the relationship.

The Money Problem

The world that your parents and grandparents grew up in, in many ways, no longer exists. When someone from an older generation says to you, "When I was your age . . . ," whatever comes after that needs to be tempered by the understanding that the social constructs that supported them are often entirely different or nonexistent today. Parents and grandparents can struggle to understand why your life looks so different than theirs did at your age. In a way they may be trying to help you solve your problems. Unfortunately this approach can be the opposite of helpful. It can feel more like criticism or judgment.

You're the best judge of your own family when it comes to whether it's even worth having the conversation about how college costs have changed or the failure of wages to keep up with the cost of living. Whether or not you decide to try to help them understand, the problem of too much debt and not enough income remains for many twentysomethings. You may have to, or choose to, rely on your family right now to help pay the bills or cover some costs. Because of this, you or they may continue to feel that reliance keeps you from being a "real" adult. It can muddy the waters about independence.

Keep in mind that a good number of your peers are in this struggle with you. A Pew Research Center analysis of Census Bureau data found that, in 2018, only 24 percent of young adults were financially independent by age twenty-two.[2] And according to a recent Pew Research Center survey, 45 percent of adults ages eighteen to twenty-nine say they have received "a lot of or some financial help from their parents" in the past twelve months.[3]

There are several ways that a twentysomething's delay in achieving financial independence can impact the relationship between parents and their adult children. Some parents may feel entitled to greater control or influence in their offspring's life.

Some young adults may feel guilty or ashamed at their lack of independence. These feelings can increase conflict, especially if communication isn't great or if your goals and your parents' goals around your finances are different. But relying on your parents financially can also open up lines of communication and mentorship. There are a few steps you can take to prevent finances from becoming a battleground:

1. Develop a plan and let your family know you have one. How much of that you share with them is up to you (especially if debating the details might create more conflict), but knowing that you have one can ease a worried parent's mind.

2. Be honest about mistakes you've made in the past and try to show that you've learned from them. If your spending has been out of control or you got in over your head on a loan or credit card, acknowledge that and assure your parents that you're trying hard to avoid making that mistake again.

3. Ask for help. In some families this may not be the best strategy, but many times parents are eager to impart their wisdom and offer guidance. Inviting them to do that can help them feel they're doing their job as parents to share what they've learned, often from having made their own mistakes.

Even the most self-sufficient among us would really struggle without some kind of family support, whether financial or emotional. The bottom line is that many twentysomethings are somewhere in between when it comes to financial independence. That doesn't mean you are not an adult. (See chapter 8 for more info about budgeting.)

TWENTYSOMETHING TALK

Financial independence is a big thing. It's also really hard when you feel the weight of debt, but it develops key life skills and earns respect to show that you can live within your means and take care of your own problems. —Bryan

Your Family Is Changing Too

Don't forget that while you have continued to grow and change, so has your family. Siblings have aged, and their lives may be changing in dramatic ways. Younger siblings especially may mourn the loss of having you in their life in the same way as when you were kids, or they may resent the independence they see you experiencing (without recognizing the increased pressure you may feel as an adult). Your parents are getting older and may be enjoying the freedoms that come with being empty nesters, or they may be struggling with a sense of loss as their identities shift and change. If your parents are divorced, there may be new living arrangements, and you may have to figure out how to relate and where you fit in this newly configured family. If you have a parent or grandparent with a health issue, you may be called on to step up in ways you haven't had to before. You may have a parent or sibling with a mental health or addiction issue. If it's dealt with openly and honestly, it may not have as big an impact on you. If it's not, it can create very complex family dynamics.

One of the tasks of our twenties is coming to terms with our families as an adult. It's healthy and emotionally mature to admit and allow that our families are not perfect, to be able to say, "My parents screwed up," but to also say, "They probably did the best they could." Our parents have strengths and weaknesses. They sometimes disappoint us. We should be able to rely on them for support, but we should also be as responsible for ourselves as we are able to be.

If there are unhealthy or abusive patterns of behavior in your family, you may need to establish a different set of boundaries. You may need to limit the time you spend with them, take time apart, or, depending on the level of harm, make an entirely clean break.

My Values Are Not Your Values

For many young adults one of the biggest points of tension is around shifts in values and belief. You may have grown up in a home where racism was tolerated or one that was extremely religious in negative and controlling ways. Your ideas about religion or politics may be different now than when you were younger. There may be a level of sexism or homophobia among your family members that you're no longer willing to tolerate. If your identity has changed in ways that your family can't or won't accept, it can be very difficult and even painful. Learn your limits with your family. Figure out which arguments you're willing to have and which ones to avoid. That's a choice you get to make as an adult.

Break the Buttons

Do you have family members who get under your skin? Who know exactly how to irritate you to your breaking point and how to push your buttons? Here's a list of seven new ways to respond that will assure those buttons stop working:

1. "I'm not talking about that today." Then don't. Change the subject or start talking to someone else.
2. "Please stop." You can add: bringing that up, joking about it, picking on me. Or just let the words stand on their own.
3. "Wow! That was mean." Sometimes you have to call it what it is.
4. If you mean no, it's okay to say no. "No, I don't want to _____." Whatever it is—I don't want to go to the place, do the thing, eat the food, help with this or that project—you're an adult. You get to decide.
5. "Are you asking me or telling me?" This one's good for family members who back you into a corner but imply you have a choice.

6. "I disagree, but that's okay. We don't have to agree to be family." There, you just became the grown-up in the conversation.

7. "Let's not fight." Depending on your tone, this could be conciliatory or a thinly veiled threat.

TWENTYSOMETHING TALK

Boundaries! I'm an adult, and just because I'm close geographically doesn't mean I spend all my free time at my parents'. Nor should I be expected to. Also, if other siblings are living farther away, siblings should be able to have sibling time without the parents being involved. I'm working on that boundary rule right now. —James

---

NOW DO THIS: Identify one thing you'd like to change about your interactions with your family. Maybe you get easily frustrated or offended. Maybe you need to be honest with them about differences in your beliefs or lifestyle. Plan to make the change and take the first step.

YOU ACTUALLY NEED TO KNOW: Learn to act on the old adage, "You can't change your family, but you can change how you react to them."

CHAPTER 10

FAST FRIENDS

The Work and Reward of Creating Your Circle

TWENTYSOMETHING TIP: Whether you're back in your hometown, staying in your college town, or moving to a new city, odds are at least some of the people you've been close to in the past are no longer geographically close. Nurturing past friendships while finding friends to connect and grow with where you are is more important than ever. It's also harder than ever. Hang in there.

Finding. the balance between staying con-nected to past friendships and continuing to seek out new ones can be really hard. It's easy to rely on those old connections. They're comfortable. You have a history together. They know you—with all your good points and bad points—and they love you. All of that counts for a lot. And you should definitely keep those connections for all those reasons. But in the life of a twenty-something, a day is bound to come when you'll need friends that are geographically close, physically there. It might be because of a move, a breakup, a lost job, or a health crisis. As much as they might want to, if your friends from the past are far away, they may not be able to show up for you.

Besides emergencies, life is just easier to manage when you have friends close by. You've got somebody to hang out with, someone to water your plants when you're away. In-town friends can pick you up at the airport. They can help you put together furniture. They can make last-minute plans. They can connect you with more friends. More important than anything is that as human beings, we need other people. We need to be able to look across the table and see that another person understands what we're going through. As corny as it sounds—we need a shoulder to cry on. In very good times or very bad times, sometimes, we just need a hug.

Friends: Get Yourself Some Good Ones

So, how do you make friends as a twentysomething? In some ways it's harder than it was when you were in school. At school you were surrounded by people you already had at least a few things in common with. Even if you were a loner, there were people your age studying some of the same things. Accidental friendships could happen at almost any moment. Now, it might be more of an effort. Depending on what your life is like, making new friends can be pretty challenging.

If you're looking for work, or you have a strange or demanding schedule, it can seem impossible to make new friends. So start with the easy stuff. Are there activities you know you want to be involved in? What interests of yours lend themselves to community and connection? Even if you only have a few extra hours a week, consider dedicating them to an activity or organization that will help you meet new people. Instead of just going to the gym, take a class or join an exercise group, run club, or team sport. Create your own art or music or robots or whatever but also connect with an organization or a group that puts on related shows, festivals, concerts, or events. Make your leisure time do double duty—recreation and relationship building. Check out our "Join up" list at the end of this chapter for activities and organizations that can help turn your free time into friend-making time.

Are you "back home" again? Don't discount friendships from the past that could be renewed. And sometimes, someone you would never have been friends with in high school can turn out to be the right friend now. Think about how much you've changed and grown since senior year. Most everyone else has too. (Not *everyone* though.) Even in a small town, new people move in, and there may be people you haven't met yet who could use a friend like you.

Look where you live. If you're in a new place, introduce yourself to people in your building. Welcome new neighbors with a note and contact info. Get to know your neighborhood by shopping, eating, and walking there. Visit the nearby parks and libraries. All these things are just first steps but will help you come across people who have at least one thing in common with you—location!

TWENTYSOMETHING TALK

The switch from living in close quarters and close community with college friends to living in a new place and/or another city, most likely without a group of friends, is really challenging. Find a place to plug into community *right away*, like a church or CrossFit gym, a swing dancing community, an ultimate frisbee group—any hobby group where people make friends, hang out, and do something is a good place to start building community. Plus, knowing that it takes about two years to "build a life" somewhere helps with the loneliness that persists longer than you want it to. —Lizza

Fighting Loneliness

A much-touted 2018 Cigna survey identified Gen Z as the loneliest generation.[1] Though many analysts are quick to point toward overuse of social media as a culprit, there was little difference found between heavy users and people with no social media use at all. Factors that can influence loneliness were identified as: sleep, time with family, physical activity, and work. Too much or too little of any of these can have a negative effect on how lonely people feel. The most important factor in fighting loneliness is regular, meaningful, in-person interactions. On one hand, that's not exactly a news flash. On the other hand, many, many people—nearly half of all Americans—report sometimes or always feeling alone. We obviously haven't figured this out yet.

As you enter your twenties and life is delivering up serious changes, loneliness can be a big deal. The very adult realization that each of us is, in some sense, alone inside our own heads and hearts is tough news. For some reason that knowledge settles in and takes hold in a new way in our twenties. Turned inside out, loneliness is a hunger for connection, a desire for that satisfying feeling of community, belonging, and meaning. When loneliness strikes, try to let it be fuel for the fire of creating new connections and cultivating the friendships you already have.

Get Closer

What if you're meeting people at work or activities but not really moving the needle from acquaintances to friends? For a lot of people, this is one of the things that seemed so much easier in earlier years. In the past you'd just spend time around people and eventually, mysteriously, you'd turn into friends. If that doesn't seem to be happening now, don't surrender to it as the new normal. Be the catalyst. Invite people over or organize an outing. Even a get-together with one or two people can move things along. If that's intimidating, ask someone to help. Then the two of you together can gather a group.

After an initial activity or two, see if the group wants to make it a regular thing—a board game night, watching the game, volunteering together, a shared meal. The benefit of regular time together—whether it's once a week or once a month—is that it gives you the forward momentum of not having to make plans every time. If it's already on everybody's calendar, it's more likely to happen. It may be weird or awkward at first, but tough it out. We tend to forget that our past friendships often had slow or awkward beginnings and only recall the closeness of the height of those friendships. Once you get through the weirdness, you'll find you have a group of people you can go to for more than just occupying your free time.

Build those tenuous connections into strong friendships. Ask for help and offer help. See if they could feed your cat while you're traveling. Offer to walk their dog at lunchtime occasionally if you work from home and they're in an office. Bring them groceries when they're sick or ask them to fix your computer or help you move furniture. Social closeness is a precursor to emotional closeness; spending time together, helping each other, can lead to supporting each other in life's tough times and transitions. From infancy we're encouraged to be independent, to literally stand on our own two feet, but only some of us are taught the value of interdependence. Interdependence means that we can count on the people around us when we need help and that they can count on us. Go ahead and build interdependence. Be someone people can count on. Go ahead and rely on others too. That's the stuff of real friendships that last over time.

TWENTYSOMETHING TALK

I think it's important to push yourself to be vulnerable with people you don't know well—tell them about your experiences and your interests. It's difficult to get close with people if they don't know anything about you. Also, I think asking people questions is always a great start. People generally enjoy talking about themselves. —Olivia

My twenties have been characterized by a lot of moving around and starting over in new cities, so I've struggled with repeatedly having to build my social network from the ground up. On top of that, each time I move, I take with me a new host of long-distance friends—mostly this is a blessing, but it is hard to leave people I love over and over again. The best part of my friendships is how much we all support each other and understand the chaos that is our twenties! —Lilly

Four Ways Volunteering Together Can Deepen a Friendship

Another way to grow closer with friends is to find activities that have a "bigger than just us" component. Passion projects, giving back, and efforts that do good can amp up a friendship in several important ways:

1. You'll gain a sense of shared purpose. The friend bond grows stronger with a common cause. Knowing that you're making a difference together suffuses the friendship with positive feelings and can elevate and intensify it.

2. You'll get to know each other better and differently. Inviting newly met friends to join you serving at the soup kitchen, coaching the kids' robotics team, or walking shelter dogs can give you the chance to see each other in a different setting and open up new conversations more connected to values and purpose.

3. You'll create positive shared memories. Today's good deeds will be tomorrow's source of pride and nostalgia. A year or two from now you'll have established a shared history of doing good and creating positive change.

4. You'll widen your circle. Finding people who care about the same things you and your new friend care about can result in even more (you guessed it) new friends.

Are Work Friends Real Friends?

Once you're employed, your social life might take a big leap forward. Now you've got a built-in set of connections. There's a set of cautions, however, that comes with those connections. As discussed in chapter 2, as far as building friendships with colleagues goes, the most important caution is to take it slow. If you're one of those people who struggles with maintaining healthy boundaries, then this one goes double for you.

Some workplaces are full of friendly people just doing their jobs and trying their best to get along with their coworkers. Others can be roiling pits of politics and backstabbing. In both types of workplaces there are people who will be friendly to you because you're new. In the first kind it's nice and can lead to ongoing friendship. In the second you might become the unwitting accomplice to, or the victim of, any number of slimy moves. Soon enough you'll have figured out the politics of your particular job: who is the boss's favorite, who is the office gossip, who does most of the work, who gets most of the credit. Until you do, though, keep your attitude friendly to all, and keep your deeply personal stories to yourself.

With that knowledge in mind, go ahead and connect with the folks you enjoy being around at work. As you begin to feel more confident about who is who, and which people you can place your trust in, try developing those friendships beyond your workplace. Those friendships can begin there, but they'll grow stronger and will be more likely to last beyond your current employment if you can nurture the connection outside of work.

TWENTYSOMETHING TALK

Take your work friendships outside of work! It's normal for friendships to start out of proximity, but if you want to keep the friendship long term, cultivate it outside of the normal environment as well. Also, your work friend might have some awesome "real-world" friends you might click with. —Beth

If You Love Being Busy

If you're working a nine-to-five job but there's not much opportunity to meet people your age or with similar interests, consider the possibility of getting a second job. It's definitely not the right solution for everyone, but if you dislike having time on your hands, look for a sideline with the specific intent of creating those connections. Keep an eye out for something that gives you face-to-face interactions and connects with the kinds of people you want to meet: working the front desk at your gym, coaching, working at a craft store, your favorite restaurant, an art gallery, or theater. A second job can get you extra income plus extra friends.

As Things Change

At this point you've most likely faced the challenge of being friends with people who are part of a couple when you're single or vice versa. As people's lives change and diverge from the comfortable sameness of all being students together to all the variations that life can take on in your twenties, it gets a lot more complex. A Pew Research Center analysis showed that, in 2016, 9 percent of people aged eighteen to twenty-four were cohabiting, 7 percent were married, 3 percent were divorced, widowed or separated, and 82 percent hadn't married. Among those aged twenty-five to thirty-four, 14 percent were cohabiting, 41 percent were married, 6 percent were divorced, widowed, or separated, and 38 percent hadn't married.[2] Most twentysomethings will have friends in each of those categories as well as friends with kids and friends without. Some people are still hammering away at their degree or remaining in academia; some have gone into the work world. You've probably started to see at least a few engagements, weddings, and babies popping up on your social media feed. It can be a little disorienting. Those big life changes come with big shifts in how friends relate to each other. No one is "ahead" of anyone else, but it's often challenging to maintain friendships as people's lives become more and more varied from one another's.

Give yourself the chance to rediscover those friendships. Continue to explore your shared memories and celebrate your past, but remember to make new memories together too. Try doing things that include significant others or children some of the time and at other times let it be just you and your friend. It may take a few tries to find out how you can continue the friendship, but if you can avoid trying to recreate the past, you'll have a much better chance at creating a future.

TWENTYSOMETHING TALK

Know that there will be an ebb and flow in friendships. But try to stay connected, even in small ways, knowing that the ebb is cyclic. Sometimes the longest friendships go through years where there's an emotional connection but not necessarily a physical one. —Maureen

One of the most difficult things to making friends in your twenties is how vastly different everyone's lives and experiences are. Some people are working "regular" nine-to-five jobs in their field of study, while some work odd jobs. Some are in school, some are in trades, some are starting a family, some are still into the "party scene." I think the most important tip to maintaining friendships in your twenties is not only to be yourself but to be understanding and flexible. A lot of friendships when you are younger feel like being inseparable from the person, but when you are in your twenties you are not always going to be able to be with one another. That is another difficulty with friendships in your twenties—realizing that not talking every day or hanging out 24–7 does not mean someone hates you or does not want to be your friend. In general, it's just about being yourself, being kind to everyone, and being understanding. —Ryan

The Introvert's Guide to Making Friends

Introverts, people who recharge by being alone, have unique challenges when it comes to friendship. Many, but not all, introverts prefer to have a smaller group of close friends. Many, but not all, introverts also tend toward shyness. That can add an extra layer of complexity to making and growing friendships. What follows here is a list of friendship pointers from introverts for introverts (pro tip: many of them will work for extroverts too):

1. **Be a joiner.** Service groups, sports teams, arts and activist organizations, churches, and Meetup groups all provide the benefit of putting you in a room full of people with whom you already have something in common. Usually there's a preset agenda and expectations are clear. What could be better?

2. **Procure a role.** You've found your group; now find a role within the group. Edit the newsletter, welcome new members, serve on the board, be their photographer. A specific role will provide more built-in interactions. If you're the one sitting at the table checking everyone in for the event, you'll meet them all with much less effort.

3. **Become an expert.** Get good at something that other people will see: teaching, dance, music, coaching, or leading. You get to "hide" behind the activity. You have the comfort level of doing something you're confident doing, and people will come to you with their questions.

4. **Host your own events in your space.** Doing what you like to do, in your own place, with the people you want to spend time with can make socializing an entirely different kind of activity.

5. **Let an extrovert adopt you.** Be a good friend to that

extroverted friend you get along well with. If you genuinely like them, chances are good you'll like some of the same people. You'll benefit by being able to connect with your friend's network and curate your own crowd from among those people.

6. **Be brave.** Challenge yourself to greet the people near you. Say "hello" instead of "excuse me." If there's someone you want to meet and you're not feeling the confidence to do it, think of your favorite extrovert and imitate that person.

7. **Prepare properly.** If you know you've got a people-y event Saturday night, try to give yourself a people-free day beforehand. Make sure you are rested and recharged before socializing.

TWENTYSOMETHING TALK

I know this sounds strange, but while I'm usually not up for going to parties, I love to host parties—it's my people in my space, therefore comfortable. —Cori

I try to schedule myself at least one social outing a month, be it with one person or a small group, via a club or local event. That keeps me in practice with meeting new people and maintaining current friendships. It's especially important with the sort of post-graduate training I had. Work can suck up all your time if you let it. —Ania

---

Consider Community

Have you ever been part of a larger organization that felt like home? A place where, even if there were ups and downs and some members came and went, there was still a sense of stability and familiarity to the group? Being part of a positive community where you can participate in a meaningful way, be welcomed and accepted for who you are, and have a chance to grow can be an incredible emotional and spiritual anchor. It could be a civic or fraternal organization, a sports group, a church, an arts group, a camp community, or something else entirely, but if you've had the experience of that kind of belonging, it almost always leaves you wanting to find that kind of connection again in your life.

If you feel that empty spot, consider yourself lucky. It's a great experience to have had. And though you're unlikely to find another group exactly like the one you miss, it's worth doing some hunting around for one that does some of those same things for you now or figuring out how to create a community that can. Try to identify the elements that were most important to you. Was it the group's sense of mission? Was it the support and friendship you discovered there? Was it because you had the opportunity to grow a skill with people supporting you and cheering you on? Once you've identified what was most valuable to you, keep that in mind as you look for places to connect in your life now. Look for welcoming groups with healthy leadership where new members have a chance to jump right in and get involved.

Community is like a well. You can keep coming back to it. As friendships wax and wane with the natural phases of people's lives, belonging to a healthy community can give you a place and a group of people to return to when friendships are in transition. At times when you're feeling a little lost, it can remind you of who you want to be. If you're struggling to find friends, consider finding a community first. It might be the best place to get both.

TWENTYSOMETHING TALK

I don't know what high school would have been like without my youth group community and my friends. I tried to find something similar at college, but the group didn't fit the bill. Then I started rowing my second semester freshman year, and I found my community! I have continued to row, and I will credit that group of friends as helping me to transition to life in a new city. I moved to Boston only knowing one person, so when I joined my rowing club a few months later, it provided the network and support I needed. The years I did AmeriCorps (right after undergrad) also provided me with a new family—especially since my programs were both residential. Finding people who have similar passions (faith, service through environmental conservation, sports) has been really important for me. —Courtney

Brainstorm places to make friends and find places to connect.

Friend-Mapping

Who you know already:

- _____

- _____

- _____

Things you like to do:

- _____

- _____

- _____

Things you want to learn:

- _____

- _____

- _____

Things you used to do and might want to start again:

- _____

- _____

- _____

People and activities related to work:

- _____

- _____

- _____

Volunteering and causes that interest you:

- _____
- _____
- _____

People you know who know a lot of people:

- _____
- _____
- _____

People and things to do near where you live:

- _____
- _____
- _____

People and things to do near where you work:

- _____
- _____
- _____

Big events that take place in your city/town:

- _____
- _____
- _____

Reach activities / crazy things you've always wanted to try:

- _____
- _____
- _____

Free Friend Dates for (Nearly) Zero Dollars

These low-cost activities with friends have a high-fun payoff:

1. **Get outdoors.** Check out your area parks, beaches, sidewalks, bike lanes, hiking trails, or nature preserves.
2. **Find free shows.** Check your local websites, social media, or paper to discover music and other entertainment that's free or only a few bucks.
3. **Eat on the cheap.** Find that cute but inexpensive diner with the rave reviews. Remember breakfast and lunch out are usually considerably less expensive than dinner. Or invite a bunch of friends over and pool your dinner dollars on delivery.
4. **Explore your neighborhood.** Find neighborhood festivals. They often feature free performances and lots to see and do.
5. **Discover discount days.** Museums and zoos often have free and discounted days. In some cities you can check out a free pass at the library.
6. **Linger longer in the library.** Of course there are books, magazines, music, and movies. But there are also classes, talks, performances, and activities.
7. **Plan a reading marathon.** Make snacks, break out your comfy clothes, and invite a few friends over. Read aloud a beloved series or classic or each read your own current favorite author. This could also be a movie marathon or video game binge.

8. **Shop the window wonderland.** You might not have much money, but it doesn't cost anything to look. Take a walk through the shopping district or your local Target to see what's new or do some preholiday reconnaissance.

9. **Be a host.** Hold a board game, trivia, or cards night; plan dish-to-pass meals or crafting days.

10. **Become a TV guide.** Get together once a week to share a show that your friend has not seen and you love (start to finish over a few weeks), then let your friend share one. Add in rotating dinner each week to amp up the fun.

11. **Swap skills.** Have a get-together where each person teaches the others something they know—how to knit, draw, read music, do yoga or (depending on space) a martial art.

12. **Complete a project.** Have a friend who wants to rearrange a room? Need to build, paint, put together furniture, or clear out your storage space? Do it together.

For more ideas on getting together with friends, see chapter 1 on living local and chapter 6 on sharing meals.

Join Up!

Many of the things you're interested in and enjoy on your own can, with small tweaks, become vehicles to friendship. Look through this list and let it be an inspiration. Your "thing" might not be here, but you might see how you can turn your solo pursuit into a communal and connecting activity.

If you like . . .	Then try . . .
Singing	Joining a choir
Playing an instrument	Joining a community band or orchestra
Drawing or painting	Taking an art class
Comedy	Joining an improv troupe or class
Politics	Volunteering for a campaign effort
History	Joining an historical society or reenactors' group
Reading	Finding a book club
Writing	Participating in a critique group or class
Dancing	Signing up for a class or learning a specific style—folk, swing, blues

Theater	Auditioning for community theater
Outdoor adventures	Looking for a local hiking group
Sports	Taking group lessons, joining a team, or coaching

NOW DO THIS: Identify three places/activities where you could meet new people. Choose one to start with and go there!

YOU ACTUALLY NEED TO KNOW: Building your network of friends can seem like a big challenge, but take it one step at a time. It can be easier than you think and will make your life better in more ways than you can count.

CHAPTER 11

YOU'RE AMAZING!

How to Find Someone Else Who Thinks So Too

TWENTYSOMETHING TIP: Whether you're already in a relationship with "the one" or you're just having fun, integrity, good boundaries, and understanding what you want out of a relationship are great guides.

Relationships are hard. Getting into them, get-
ting out of them, and sustaining them takes time, energy, and
attention. For many people, though certainly not everyone, marriage
and family are eventual goals. For these and many other reasons,
there's a lot of pressure to be in a relationship—or at least to be looking for one. Now may be the right time for you. Or it might not be. If
other parts of your life are unsettled—work, education, finances—
being in a steady, supportive relationship can be a real stabilizing
force. Are you in a relationship and that's how it functions for you?
Great. Carry on. But relationships can also be distracting, disrup-
tive, and sometimes even destructive. Take the time to assess the
impact of your dating or relationship on the rest of your life. Make
choices that match well with your overall goals and values.

If you're not in a relationship right now, think about whether
or not you want to be. Inevitably, and probably multiple times, the
question, *To date or not to date?* will come up, and it's good to have
thought about what you want beforehand. Do you just want someone to go out with occasionally? A once-in-a-while hangout? Are
you looking for a serious relationship or something short term?
Why do you need to ask yourself all these questions? Because if
you want to avoid hurting other people and getting hurt yourself,
it's important to be honest about what you want. And you can't be
honest with anyone else until you've been honest with yourself.

If you do decide you want to be actively looking, keep in mind
there are lots of different ways to meet people. Online dating sites

can be a great way to match up with people of similar interests; more couples now meet online than through any other means.[1] It's also a convenient way to meet people when you're in a new place and you're just beginning to build social networks. The other big benefit to meeting people online is that, unlike at a party, work, or in recreational groups, you know everyone else is there looking, just like you.

All that said, don't overlook those other opportunities. Nearly all the places we discussed in chapter 10 to find and build friendships are also good places to look for romantic relationships. Getting "fixed up" by friends can have its downsides, but the people you know and like often know other people you'll also like. Connecting with someone to date through friends or common activities can lower the pressure to prove yourself. You already know some of the same people and travel in some of the same circles. Sometimes even that little bit of common ground can be a big confidence booster.

It can be discouraging and tiring to continue to date and to try to maintain a positive attitude of hope and possibility. There are people in the world who will be attracted to you. If you have a hard time believing this, or if you keep ending up with people who hurt or betray you, address those things head-on. If you find yourself getting discouraged or cynical, you might need to give yourself a break for a bit and come back to dating when you can approach it with a little optimism.

In the Beginning

The early stages of a relationship are a balancing act. You don't want to get ahead of yourself, but you also don't want to hold back and risk losing something that could be really great. Be honest with the person you're dating. If you're not looking for anything serious right now, you owe it to them, and to yourself, to be up front about that. You may change your mind later, but you can cross that bridge if you come to it. Early on it's easy to confuse attraction with love. As human beings we are wired for connection—emotional and physical—but physical intimacy is not a universal language. Let me say it again: physical intimacy is not a universal language. One person's giving and sharing of themselves is another person's scratching an itch.

Be sure to use verbal communication along with physical communication to stay in sync with your partner and avoid hurting someone or getting hurt yourself. This includes being clear about consent. Seek verbal consent as a new relationship becomes physically intimate. Enthusiastic consent—not just the absence of a no but the presence of an unequivocal yes—is what you should be looking for as your emotional intimacy becomes physical intimacy. Give respect and get respect. If the other person is crossing boundaries, say so. If they don't listen, consider it an early warning sign. If they're not giving you respect now, think about what that might look like down the road.

TWENTYSOMETHING TALK

Give them space and value them for who they are. Be a good listener. Be open about the things you love about them and realize you won't be able to change the things you don't like. Someone fun and positive is simply irresistible. —Sofia

Don't force the big conversations until, at the earliest, the third date, or whenever you really start to feel feelings for a person. Having these conversations too early can be a red flag. —Marcus

I've valued each of us having a strong sense of integrity and empathy and always being up-front about issues that may arise. I've been in a relationship for almost three years, and one of the things I have valued most over the last few years is being able to share laughter and just be around the person I most care about without fear of judgment.—Austin

What If It's the Real Thing?

Real love can take us by surprise. It can come along when we're not looking and when it's not convenient. It can be an incredible feeling. We talk about love's ability to sweep you off your feet. We say things like, "You're head over heels." There's a reason we have all those dramatic metaphors for falling in love. Love can upend your life and expectations. It is exciting and scary all at the same time. Having the courage to be vulnerable to and with another person can pay off in the biggest way. It's not bad to be a little cautious though. When things don't go as planned or the person we've fallen for turns out to not be the person we'd imagined they were, it hurts. So follow your heart, but take your brain with you.

As you fall, keep in touch with the people who know and love you best. Those people can provide a little braking power as the roller coaster of feelings has you rushing up and down hills. They can be your reality check. It's natural that you'll be spending more time with the new person in your life, but keep up with family and friends. Make time for yourself and your own hobbies—both as a matter of self-protection in case the relationship doesn't hold up and as a way to establish healthy patterns within the relationship of each of you having time to yourselves.

Love can happen when we're still hurting from a previous relationship or when we're experiencing sorrow from a big loss or setback. Many bereavement guides and most recovery programs caution against getting into a serious relationship (or forbid dating altogether) because they recognize that to be in a healthy relationship, you need two healthy people. People who are grieving, in recovery from addiction or trauma, or working their way back from a mental health crisis are not, by definition, their healthiest selves. It can be hard at times to figure out if something that looks and feels like love is just a safety ring tossed to someone who's drowning. If you find yourself suddenly in over your head emotionally, don't be afraid to sort it through with a trusted friend, mentor, or therapist.

How to Be a Good Partner

Getting what you need in a relationship and paying attention to what your partner needs from you sounds a lot easier than it is at times. At the beginning of a relationship, people are often on their best behavior. They're working hard to communicate, to figure out what the other person likes and what makes them happy. Early on, while there's a lot of energy and motivation around the relationship, it's easy to overlook some of the problems. It's not a bad thing to do, either, especially as you adjust to another person's preferences and they're getting used to yours. Just don't let it become a habit. If something the other person is doing is making you unhappy, you owe it to yourself and them to communicate this as kindly but as forthrightly as you can. If the person you're with is trying to tell you about what they want or need, listen and try not to be defensive.

Couples in their twenties disagree, sometimes a lot. It's not necessarily a bad thing because it can be a sign that you're working on the issues that will help you stay together long term. Twentysomethings fight about commitment to the relationship, about how much time they should spend together, about jealousy, about sex, about what the standard of cleanliness for living space should be and who should maintain it. They fight about the future, they fight about being listened to, about hurt feelings, about a loss of romance, about their friends and who to spend time with as a couple, about each other's personal habits, about money, about relatives, and that's not all!

Disagreeing isn't a problem, but it's important to learn to fight fair. No put-downs or ridicule. Be honest and engage in the discussion. Stick to the matter at hand (no dragging out old faults or mistakes). Listen and seek to understand the other person's perspective rather than trying to "win" an argument. Winning a fight with someone you love means the person you love lost, and that's not good. You might not feel good after a disagreement, but hopefully each of you understands the other person's perspective a little more.

TWENTYSOMETHING TALK

I have a fun way of asking my current girlfriend how she feels by asking in jest about the "progress report" on the relationship. I would do this monthly in the beginning as a way to humorously open up our conversation to talking about the relationship. —Marcus

I try to notice what my partner does for me and do the same for him. I really value being listened to, so I also try to listen. Some of the most important things are talking often, being open about things that bother me, and starting statements with "I feel . . ." instead of "you always . . .". Having a mature and serious partner is comforting and encourages me to push myself. —Molly

Patience! I am struggling with this so much right now. For me, I was single for so long, and then when we started dating we went from zero to one hundred so quickly. I also lose patience quickly and tend to say "stupid" things without thinking. I do this to the people who are closest to me, unfortunately. —Tyler

How Honest Should You Be?

Being honest doesn't mean always revealing your entire self to everyone all the time. That wouldn't be smart or safe. There are parts of yourself, your history and identity, your successes and hurts, that people are only entitled to know after they've shown themselves to be dedicated to your well-being and worthy of your trust. Honesty should ramp up in tandem with emotional intimacy. If you're getting close with someone you're dating but feeling like you can't be honest with them about what you want or need, take time to assess that response. Is it because you have a hard time trusting in general or because the other person doesn't seem trustworthy? Either way it's an important issue to learn to navigate.

Many people have a hard time with trust. Opening up to another person can be scary if you're newer to relationships, if you've been hurt in the past, or if you've got a family history of complicated or harmful relationships. You may have some emotional work of your own to do before you can go deeper into a relationship with another person. Reading, skill building, therapy, and looking at your past relationship patterns can all be helpful when it comes to getting better at trust, honesty, and communication. Ultimately, to be a person of integrity is to be someone whose behaviors match very closely with their beliefs.

Healthy Boundaries How-To

Creating and maintaining healthy boundaries in a relationship is important, but it's not always easy. Finding the right "settings" at each point in the relationship takes knowing ourselves, having the courage and self-esteem to be honest about what we want, and getting to know our partners. Learning to be both independent and interdependent takes practice. Briefly described, healthy boundaries look like this:

- each person getting time to themselves
- each person getting to be themselves, including having their own beliefs, opinions, preferences, and friends
- each person being responsible for themselves
- each person feeling like they can ask for what they need and can count on the other person to do the same
- neither person demanding their own way or allowing themselves to always be the one to accommodate the other—instead seeking compromise

Having these limits keeps a relationship from wandering into an unhealthy territory where one person is a doormat for the other person to walk all over. In a relationship without healthy boundaries, people are not emotionally safe, and sometimes they aren't even physically safe. Manipulation and coercion can replace freedom and independence. Establishing and maintaining healthy boundaries helps couples strengthen their relationship over time and be sure each person's needs are being met.

TWENTYSOMETHING TALK

It's unreasonable to expect someone to be your everything: your lover, your best friend, your dance partner, your cheerleader. That's what the rest of your support system is there for. It takes a village for all of us. —Sofia

Be honest, but don't give up whole pieces of yourself to people who won't appreciate that. There are people who won't pick up the pieces you offer them, and that can feel devastating. You learn how to tell who will care for you and who won't. —Jackie

The biggest thing to be honest about, I think, is health—mental and physical. Are you sick? Do you have an STI or condition that they should have context about in case anything were to happen? Be up-front. Same with mental health. It's good to lean on your friends for support as well, but your partner should be aware of your body and mindset if you are intimate. —Morgan

Opting Out

Waiting to be in a relationship, waiting to date, or not dating at all are legitimate options, regardless of what your best friend, your mother, or anyone else might say. You know yourself, and you'll know when the time is right for you, if it ever is; remaining single is a totally viable option. For some people, opting out of the dating scene is related to cultural expectations or religious norms. For others it can be a matter of self-preservation. After a messy breakup or a big disappointment, while you're grieving a loss, in the early stages of recovery of any kind, or if you're dealing with another big life change, it's important to tune into your own heart and mind. Take care of yourself. When you're dealing with a major peak or valley in your life story, it's not the time to risk your well-being. Not only that, in times like those, your emotional energy might be all spent. If you've got nothing left to give to a potential partner, holding off on trying to start a new relationship is a wise move for your sake and the sake of the other person.

There are big benefits to opting out of dating and relationships. It can be less expensive. You have more time for your friends, projects, causes, and interests. You can make your own choices without compromise about how you spend your free time, when you visit your family, and what your priorities are. You may find you're steadier emotionally without another person's happiness and approval to worry about. If you love your work, you can dive into it without feeling guilty that you're shortchanging your significant other.

The downsides can be mitigated. If you find yourself lonely, make sure that you're tending your friendships and family relationships. If you're feeling self-conscious in social situations, find another single who will be your plus one. If you love eating out but don't like doing it alone, invite a friend or try having lunch out instead of dinner. There tend to be more single diners at lunchtime. Try to have open conversations with friends about your choice to be on your own. Letting them know you still want to be social in your singlehood can ease worries about socializing with couples.

TWENTYSOMETHING TALK

I'd much rather be single than dating someone who isn't right for me.
—Laurel

I've never opted out of dating purposely. I *have* had periods of time where I was not actively dating. Those periods came naturally—I didn't have to try to make them happen. —Priya

I was single for nearly six years after dating from my late teens to mid/late twenties nonstop. My last few relationships were unhealthy—there was no trust, and I had a mindset that everyone I would date was like that. I needed to take a step back and focus on myself, my career, and my own interests, such as traveling. I think this was like hitting the reset button and allowed me to forgive and forget those relationships. I will admit that there were times when it was not easy; I wanted the comfort of having someone near me and someone to talk to, but this was something I had to do in order to have healthy future relationships. —Tyler

NOW DO THIS: Who in your life has given you the best relationship advice? Have a conversation with that person about where you're at right now.

YOU ACTUALLY NEED TO KNOW: Love is complex, but also amazing. So are you. If you're willing to do the hard work of being in a relationship, you can reap the benefits. If you're not, that's okay too. Just be honest with yourself and others about it.

PART 4

SELF-CARE SYMPOSIUM

CHAPTER 12

THE GOOD NEWS ABOUT YOUR BAD HABITS

TWENTYSOMETHING TIP: Often the bad habits we had as kids or teenagers start to catch up with us in our twenties. The good news is bad habits can be broken and good ones can take their place.

What's the bad habit that causes the most problems for you? Or the one you thought you'd kicked but comes back to pounce on you when you're down? Maybe you drink a little more than you'd like or have trouble going to bed at a reasonable hour. Are you a procrastinator or disorganized? Do you forget to take your meds? Spend too much money? Maybe junk food is your guilty pleasure or you're addicted to social media. If any of those is true, you've come to the right place.

What about good habits? Are there some you have come by pretty naturally and you just don't have to think much about? Are you pretty good at eating a balanced diet or getting places on time? Maybe you grew up learning how to keep things clean and orderly and you do it out of habit, without having to think much about it. That's the blessing, and curse, of habits. Once well-formed they can carry us along without us having to decide every time to do the hard things. The good news about bad habits is that habits can change. You can replace a destructive habit with one that makes your life better.

Habits Rule (But Not Always in a Good Way)

In many ways, adolescence is terrible preparation for young adulthood. From the fluctuating hormones to the variable sleep patterns, the often-terrible eating habits to the sometimes-volatile relationship shifts—all these elements may need a hard reset for twentysomething life. Habits around sleep, food, physical activity, emotions, and relationships are important for maintaining both physical and mental health. Important, but not particularly easy to change. Many people spend their teenage years with parents coaching (or nagging) them about all those things and more. In some ways twentysomething life is about learning to become your own coach (or nag) on all those habits. Here's some of the what and why of all that:

1. **Sleep.** Most people need eight hours. Some people can survive on less, some need more. Figure out what your allotment is and how to get it. A lack of good sleep can cause problems with attention, decision-making, mood, appetite, and more. Getting enough good sleep can make you more productive and more creative; it can also improve your mood and your overall health.

2. **Relationships.** It's easy to let too much time go by and, in the busyness of life, let our important relationships go untended. Be in the habit of keeping in touch with friends and family, spending time in person or whatever version of the next best thing works for you (text, phone, video chat). Staying connected helps us feel anchored, known, and whole.

3. **Food.** Move toward eating regularly and well. You can pick up good habits around food to replace skipping meals, overeating, or eating too much of the things that leave you feeling sluggish or gross (see chapter 6 for more details).

4. **Physical activity.** Having an exercise habit—something you do every day or on set days each week—can make a huge difference in how you feel. Even adding a little more activity to your day helps. As you start to look at bad habits you want to eliminate, consider subbing in one of these positive habits: walking, stretching, yoga, or other workouts.

5. **Health.** One of the hardest habits to break (but with some of the best benefits if you can do it) is smoking. If you're still tanning, or if you're not careful about sun exposure, change that habit and save your skin, literally. Health habits to develop: wear your seat belt every time, wear a helmet when participating in sports with high head-injury rates, be protective of your sexual health, and get healthcare. Use your health benefits if you have them. If you don't, find a clinic or look up low-cost options for doctors and dentists.

6. **Emotions.** Learn to recognize your patterns. If you're a grudge holder or a comparison junkie, if you're hotheaded or prone to jealousy, all of those emotions and thought patterns are habits you can learn to step back from. Hitting pause and observing your own feelings can provide you with a safety line, a way out of the trap of negative emotions than can destroy relationships and drag you under emotionally. You can develop new habits around dealing with your anger and being a grown-up about conflict.

There are plenty of other habits that twentysomethings complain about having a hard time breaking: procrastinating, not keeping up with cleaning and laundry, spending too much time in front of a screen and not enough time in person, overspending and under-saving, eating out too much, not sticking up for themselves, overcommitting or having a hard time saying no, not taking good care of expensive stuff so it lasts longer (everything from cars to computers), paying bills on time. Many twentysomethings know the good habits they'd like to have but don't always know how to develop them.

TWENTYSOMETHING TALK

It takes longer than people think to change a habit. Most people don't give it the right amount of time or take it slow enough to stick. —Siri

I use my phone to help remind me to follow through on changing a habit and slowly cut back how much it reminds me. —Marcus

Be intentional. Good habits can be maintained by thinking about them and how you will continue to practice them. By setting aside time, space, and mental capacity for your good habits, you will see yourself doing them more. —Marisa

---

Breaking a Bad Habit

There are many (many!) popular books, websites, and social media resources on breaking bad habits and forming good ones. It's worth looking through some of that to consider what might work best for you. Try the "one small thing" method. Let's say your bedroom is a mess. That pile of dirty dishes and books and tissues and who knows what else on your nightstand is spilling over onto the floor. There's dirty laundry everywhere and nothing is "where it belongs." You're sick of living in disorganization but feel overwhelmed about how to go from pigsty to pristine. At some point you'll need to do a big cleanup, but for now, try just clearing off your nightstand. Even if bringing the dirty dishes out makes a mess in the kitchen instead and you have to stuff the books under the bed, make that nightstand your little shrine of organization. Decide right then what's allowed to stay there. Maybe it's one book, your water bottle, and your charger. Set yourself up for success and be strict about what those few items might be.

Now pick a time of day for the next week that you'll clear everything off that isn't those few things—dishes to the kitchen, trash in the trash can, and maybe even wipe it down with a cloth (or a dirty sock)—and try to keep it up for the whole week. If you're good in the morning, do it then. If it's easier to make that quick cleanup part of your bedtime routine, go for it! If you're doing it every day, it shouldn't take more than five minutes.

Once you've done it for a week, assess your progress. Try doing it for a second week. Then if you can do it for a whole month, maybe reward yourself by getting a small treat (a new trash can perhaps?) that brightens that space and reinforces your progress. Try applying the "one small thing" method to any habit you have that gets under your skin. Choose one small thing you won't procrastinate about, one small thing you'll stop overspending on, or one small bill you'll always pay on time.

Is Anxiety to Blame?

If you scratch the surface of many of the most common bad habits, right underneath you'll find anxiety. Procrastination struggles, binge drinking, disordered eating, self-sabotage (both at work and in relationships), and too much screen time—all of these habits (and others) can have their roots in anxiety. Part of breaking these habits is recognizing where they're coming from. Dr. Timothy Pychyl of Carleton University, when talking about procrastination, said that it's "not a time-management problem, it's an emotion-management problem."[1] You can learn to identify the feelings that prompt these habits, and once you start recognizing them, you can do something else with them instead of engaging in the habit you want to break. Similar to the method of replacement described above, when you catch yourself beginning to engage in whatever the habit is, stop and check your emotions. There are several different practices you can substitute: mindfulness practices, self-compassion, and grounding techniques, to name a few.

TWENTYSOMETHING TALK

It's easier to revert back to what you know because it's comfortable. Even if it is harming you. —Siri

When I get anxious I procrastinate doing my work because I don't want to do it, but it only creates more anxiety. —Kay

Is It Just a Bad Habit?
Or Something More?

Bad habits can cause trouble for us. It's worth trying to beat a bad habit because our lives can improve and we're usually happier when we're able to exchange a bad habit for a good one. But what about the times when we can't? A bad habit like being messy or staying up too late doesn't usually cause enough trouble that life becomes unmanageable. But a bad habit like binge drinking or gambling can start to have pretty serious consequences as it spins out of control. So how do you know if what started out as a bad habit has slipped over the edge into a new category?

According to *Psychology Today*, "A person with an addiction uses a substance, or engages in a behavior, for which the rewarding effects provide a compelling incentive to repeat the activity, despite detrimental consequences."[2] Simply put, a bad habit is annoying and problematic; an addiction is destructive and impairing. What is important to remember is that addictions don't start out destructive. The kinds of things we get addicted to often begin with a high level of pleasure and satisfaction. People can become addicted to (or have use disorders or excessive behavior patterns around) all kinds of things: gambling, porn, sex, alcohol, drugs, shopping, eating, video games, and more.

Addictions escalate. The thing that at one point gave us relief and escape shifts over into feelings of hopelessness, failure, shame, and guilt as it starts to destroy our relationships, our health, our jobs, and our finances. Other defining components of addiction are reduced self-control over the behavior, compulsive engagement in it, and a craving state prior to engaging in it.[3] Many addictions have an underlying mental health condition like depression or anxiety that prompted a person to seek relief in the first place. In more recent years treatment for addiction or substance use disorder is seen as part of an overall mental health treatment plan rather than a separate component. This kind of treatment has high levels of effectiveness.

Quitting doesn't always take the first time; replacing the addiction with a positive alternative and tending to any underlying mental health issues or past trauma will help tremendously. If you can quit once, you can quit again; keep quitting until you've quit all the way.

. . . .

NOW DO THIS: Choose one habit that you'd like to kick. Write down two things you can do to start kicking it. For example: I want to stop staying up too late. So (1) for one week I'll write down what I did the evening before and what time I went to bed and (2) the next week I'll start turning off my screens an hour before I need to be asleep.

YOU ACTUALLY NEED TO KNOW: Bad habits can keep us from becoming the people we hope to be, but if we're willing to face them, change is possible.

CHAPTER 13

HOW'S YOUR BRAIN DOING?

Mental Health for Twentysomethings

TWENTYSOMETHING TIP: Knowing what helps and what hurts in the struggle for mental health is half the battle. Learn how to take good care of your brain so it can take good care of you.

Before we talk about mental illness, let's talk about what it looks like to be mentally well. If you're well, you're getting enough sleep, but not too much, at the times you need to. For most people that means sleeping at night and being awake during the day. If you are mentally healthy you are eating enough, but not too much, of a variety of (fairly) nutritious foods. You get some physical activity in a few times a week, you have relationships and activities you enjoy, and you experience a range of emotions but aren't stuck in any particular mode. When you experience a setback or loss you might feel down for a while, but you have a sense that, before long, you'll feel better. And you know there are steps you can take to help you move toward feeling better.

For someone with a mental illness, one or more of those things can be disrupted or completely out of control. If you've ever suspected you might be struggling with a mental health issue, or if you already have a diagnosis, then you might recognize something on that list that wasn't (or isn't) going so well. If anxiety or depression or some other mental health issue is interfering with any of those activities listed above and you haven't already talked with a doctor or therapist about it, it might be time to start thinking about that. It can be scary to face mental health head-on, especially if you've never seen someone deal with their mental health in positive ways or ways that don't involve shame and embarrassment. The positive results of taking action, though, can literally save your life.

Assessing My Own Mental Health

Everyone gets down sometimes. It's true. But that's also what we sometimes tell ourselves when we don't feel like facing the reality of a mental health issue. So how does a person know if their current thought patterns are just something they are going through temporarily or a sign of something more serious? First, try finding out a little more about mental illness and the associated symptoms from reliable sources such as the National Alliance on Mental Illness (www.nami.org/home) and the National Institute of Mental Health (www.nimh.nih.gov/index.shtml). Second, keep an eye out for signs that might indicate something more serious is going on. Signs might include:

- excessive worrying or fear
- feeling excessively sad or low
- confused thinking or problems concentrating and learning
- extreme mood changes, including uncontrollable "highs" or feelings of euphoria
- prolonged or strong feelings of irritability or anger
- avoiding friends and social activities

- difficulties understanding or relating to other people
- changes in sleeping habits or feeling tired and low energy
- changes in eating habits such as increased hunger or lack of appetite
- changes in sex drive
- difficulty perceiving reality (delusions or hallucinations, in which a person experiences and senses things that don't exist in objective reality)
- inability to perceive changes in one's own feelings, behavior, or personality ("lack of insight" or anosognosia)
- overuse of substances like alcohol or drugs
- multiple physical ailments without obvious causes (such as headaches, stomachaches, vague and ongoing "aches and pains")
- thinking about suicide
- inability to carry out daily activities or handle daily problems and stress
- an intense fear of weight gain or concern with appearance[1]

If any (or several) of the signs and symptoms sound familiar, you may be dealing with a mental health issue. If your day-to-day life and relationships are disrupted, or if your mood, thinking, or behavior is impacted by what you're experiencing, take the next step and talk to your doctor about getting assessed, or find a therapist yourself.

The Courage to Address It

Taking that next step can be hard. Many people avoid dealing with their mental health in straightforward ways. Often they don't even realize they're avoiding it. The stigma associated with mental illness has gotten much better in the last few decades, but it's still a very real problem. If mental illness was never discussed in your family, or worse, if it was equated with weakness or failure, it can be an uphill battle getting past that sense of shame. Mental illness, like any other illness, should never be blamed on the person who has it. Blaming someone for being ill is, at best, uninformed and in many cases counterproductive. One of the best things you can do to begin with is learn more about mental health and learn to take good care of yourself. If you're trying to help someone else you care about who is struggling with mental health, the same applies. For most mental health issues there's not a cure, but there are many treatments and strategies for coping that can make a big difference in how a person feels and how well they are able to function.

Having the courage to deal with your mental health may require you to unlearn some misinformation you may have been exposed to. Mental illness can have several different causes. There are genetic factors—it can run in families. It can be influenced by past or present trauma. There are physical illnesses that can cause mental health issues or make them worse. Whatever the cause, it's worth pursuing treatment. Getting mental health treatment and learning to take steps to protect your mental health can make everyday life easier to handle, improve your relationships, reduce mental health crises, and even help prevent mental illness from getting worse.

If there are people in your life who seem embarrassed to talk with you about getting help or are reluctant to support you in your effort to get help, then find some people who aren't. No one should make you feel bad about trying to improve your mental health. You aren't alone. Each year, one in five American adults experiences mental illness.[2] More and more people are realizing that it's okay to talk about and treat their mental illness just as they would any other illness.

TWENTYSOMETHING TALK

I found my therapist by calling the number for our EAP (employee assistance program) through my work. They gave me three free sessions and two recommendations for local therapists who accept my insurance. Super easy, and I would highly suggest anyone use it if their employer offers it! —Alex

Ask your friends if they know anyone good. Check the internet. If you're at a university, they probably have services or lists of outside providers. Mental. Health. Is. Critical. —Lilly

---

Finding Help

Once you've done a little reading or research, the next step is talking to your doctor. If you don't have a doctor or clinic you go to but you're working, see if your job has an EAP (employee assistance program) and try that number. If you're in school, there may be a counseling center on your campus where you can get connected or referred. Many cities and counties have mental health hotlines where you can get help finding a doctor or therapist. If you're concerned about the cost, seek out a practitioner who offers a sliding scale fee (you make less, you pay less). Most health insurance providers offer some coverage, and in some states mental health visits are covered at the same rates as other health care.

Do It Now

Depending on where you live, it can take a while to get in to see a doctor or therapist. Many towns and cities have a severe shortage of mental health practitioners, so even if you start to feel better before your appointment, don't cancel! Keep the appointment and report how you were feeling and why you were seeking help. That will establish you as a patient, then if you run into trouble down the road, you've already made that connection.

Treatment Options

Your doctor or therapist may recommend a support group, counseling, medication, learning some new skills, or some combination of those things. Some people experience dramatic improvements quickly. For other people, change comes more slowly. Be patient with yourself and your treatments. Some people are reluctant to take medications at first and admittedly, side effects can be tough to handle. It can also take time for you and your doctor to sort out the right medications for you at the right doses. You may get pushback from friends or family about meds. There are very few people who would tell someone that they didn't need to take insulin for their diabetes or get their cancer treated, but for some reason people feel free to do that with mental health treatment. It's often out of fear or ignorance. Try not to get discouraged. Most people find that treatment helps.

What Else Can I Do?

In addition to getting to a doctor or therapist, there are lots of options and possibilities when it comes to caring for your mental health. As you try different things, you'll find some have a big impact and are worth the effort or expense and others may not help much. What works for someone else may not work for you—at least right now. Keep track of what works so that when you hit a wall you can go back to your "what works" list and try something from there. Here are a few suggestions to get you started:

1. **Build your network.** Surround yourself with people who can help and support you. Find the friends and family members who are willing to be there for you when times are hard and encourage you when you are starting to struggle. Some of these people will be online, but be sure you have some that are geographically close who can help you in a crisis.

2. **Take a walk.** Even a tiny bit of activity can influence mood. A daily walk or exercise routine can be a stabilizing factor for some people. Even if you're not an "exercise

person," try to add a little movement to your day and see if it helps.

3. **Form good habits.** When you have a habit or routine that influences your mental health positively, that's one less thing you have to decide to do each day for yourself because it's already part of your routine. Revisit chapter 12 to see how to do it.

4. **Focus on sleep.** If you find yourself feeling crabby, run-down, or depressed, check your sleep schedule. If you have a habit of staying up too late, remember this piece of advice: if you wouldn't get up early to do this (watch this next episode, play this next round, argue on social media for another half hour) don't stay up to do it. Our self-control tends to be worst late in the day, so recognize that and put yourself to bed.

5. **Have an outlet.** Art, music, sports, gaming, caring for a pet, being part of a volunteer organization—any of these can help maintain good mental health.

6. **Eat well.** Eating poorly can be both symptom and cause when it comes to mental illness. When you're not doing well, you tend not to eat as well. Eating poorly or erratically can make you feel worse. The closer you can get to a regular eating schedule with good, healthy food the better. If you experience panic attacks, try hard not to skip meals. It will help you avoid the big drops in blood sugar that can put you at risk for more panic attacks.[3] If you struggle with food and weight issues or if you've already been diagnosed with an eating disorder, then you might

already have strategies in place that help. If not, therapy, nutrition counseling, support groups, and medications can all be effective.

7. **Watch out for toxic people.** You know who they are. They leave you feeling drained or exhausted or judged or small. If they are people you must spend time with, try to prepare yourself ahead of time with good rest and good food and something that makes you feel good about yourself (time with a pet or favorite person or doing something you're good at). Limit the amount of time and give yourself a recovery hour afterward if you can. If you can eliminate these folks from your life or dramatically reduce the contact you have with them, all the better.

8. **Avoid triggering media, places, and activities.** Don't go see that movie or hang out at the breakup site. If loud music or flashing lights or whatever is a trigger for you, avoid it. Tell someone you trust that that's your plan so they can help if you're getting pressure to participate in something that you know is destructive for you.

9. **Keep learning.** Learning new things in general can be a great mood lifter. A new skill or working to get better at something you already enjoy can help with self-esteem and insulate against negative thought patterns.

10. **Be mindful.** Mindfulness practices like meditation, prayer, yoga, and other practices that teach focus and attention can help with mental health.

11. **Be aware.** If you and the people close to you can start to take note of the things that tend to destabilize your

mental health, it can help you take better care of yourself over the long haul. Many people find that skimping on sleep, overdoing socializing during the holidays, getting overcommitted with work or projects, or simply forgetting to give yourself downtime can have negative effects. Conversely, going too long without socializing or connecting with supportive people can also cause problems.

12. **Give yourself a break.** If things don't go as you had hoped or you're not able to keep a commitment or reach a goal, keep in mind that you can try another day and that there are lots of different ways to be successful. Learn to forgive yourself and deal with the grief that can come along with having a mental health issue. You'll miss events occasionally. You'll disappoint other people sometimes. Just as with any other chronic illness, you can't always control how you'll be doing on any given day.

Who Can You Talk To?

Think about the last time someone told you about a running injury or a cancer diagnosis. Were they ashamed or embarrassed? No? Was there a lot of self-blame or secrecy surrounding it? Probably not. We haven't always been open about things like cancer or other deadly illnesses, but these days it's pretty normal for folks to discuss illnesses taking place in their bodies. Now imagine the same conversation but the problem is a mental health issue. Would it go the same? Someday we may be able to talk about what's going on with our brains as easily as we do what's going on with our bodies. The stigma, the vulnerability, the hang-ups that we still have around mental illness can make being open about it really complicated. At the same time, we know that social support can make a tremendously positive difference when it comes to mental health outcomes.[4]

If being open about mental illness is new to you, choose your circle slowly and wisely. Test the waters with your most trusted family member or friend. Over time you'll learn to answer people's questions and help educate them about what's going on with you without feeling rattled or defensive. There will probably be people in your life with whom you never or rarely share how you're doing because they have shown limited capacity for empathy or support regarding your mental health. That's fine. They are not your responsibility or your problem. If there are people you are uncertain about but would like to be able to talk to, invite them to do some reading about mental health first and then try having an initial conversation. You are not obligated to educate anyone else about mental health and should not have to explain or defend yourself. If you choose to share information and someone reacts badly or hurtfully, give yourself some distance from that person.

TWENTYSOMETHING TALK

I'm open about my mental health struggles, but I'm a psychology student, so perhaps I'm biased. It's a stigmatized topic, and it's up to us to help it be less so. No one is obligated to share beyond what they want, but I believe that openly sharing our struggles and being vulnerable with others is the key to building lasting relationships. —Lilly

I'm pretty much an open book around anyone, except my fiancé is the only person who really knows I've had suicidal thoughts. I feel like people just wouldn't know what to say if I told them, and it would be too uncomfortable. —Alex

Your close friends are great assets. Get together with a couple close friends at someone's place, enjoy a few drinks, and talk with each other and check in. Share what you feel comfortable sharing. Lots of people are going through the same things, so choose people you feel comfortable sharing with. —Jamie

I only talk to my closest friends, whom I know I can trust, but I think we really need to lose the stigma that seeing a therapist is a bad thing. —Kay

Getting Through a Bad Day or a Bad Month

If you feel depression, anxiety, mood swings, or any other mental health issue creeping up on you, don't wait. Take action right away to help yourself cope. Here are some survival tips to get you through a mental health rough patch:

1. Make a list of safe people and let them know how you're feeling. By alerting your people now you set off a system where people who care about you will check up on you in the weeks ahead. You can even ask them specifically to do that.

2. Ask those same people for help. You can ask for anything from just keeping you company to help with everyday tasks like laundry or cooking. Know that when you're doing better you can return the favor.

3. Set your priorities and cancel plans that don't fall within them. Cut back on the things that might be too much to manage right now.

4. Get your survival tools together. Make sure you've got your meds and prep for time at home with groceries and supplies.

5. If you can, see your doctor or therapist. Many mental health professionals keep a few slots open or will squeak an emergency appointment in at lunchtime or the end of their day. You can ask at one of your regular appointments what the policy is. If you don't know, call and ask if they have emergency appointments or ask for their "next available" appointment.

6. Simplify your routines, from clothing and laundry to personal hygiene. (Febreze is your friend! So is dry shampoo.)

7. If you have the kind of job that allows you to work from home, set that up in advance so you won't have to show up at the office when you're bottoming out.

Suicidal Thoughts

The clinical name for thoughts of death or suicide is suicidal ideation. Just "hoping to not wake up again" or wishing you weren't around are also considered suicidal thinking. For some people, these thoughts come and go. For others they can be a relentless pattern. If you are having thoughts of suicide—whether milder feelings of "I just don't want to be here" or more specific thoughts of death—talk to your doctor or therapist or to a friend who can help you advocate for yourself.

Suicide rates are at an all-time high among young adults. Part of the increase is because we are keeping better track of deaths caused by suicide, but that only accounts for a portion of the dramatic 56 percent rise in the suicide rate between 2007 and 2017 among Americans aged ten to twenty-four years old.[5] That's why, even though suicidal ideation is a hard topic to talk about, it's a conversation worth having.

Suicidal ideation is actually a symptom of other mental health issues and is treatable. There are medications and therapies that specifically help reduce and eliminate it. Unfortunately, it's a real danger and needs to be taken seriously. Here are some factors that increase a person's risk of dying by suicide:[6]

- **a family history of suicide**
- **substance use** (drugs can create mental highs and lows that worsen suicidal thoughts)
- **intoxication** (more than 1 in 3 people who die from

suicide are under the influence of alcohol at the time of death)[7]

- **access to firearms**
- **a serious or chronic medical illness**
- **gender** (more women than men attempt suicide, but men are nearly four times more likely to die by suicide)[8]
- **a history of trauma or abuse**
- **prolonged stress**
- **a recent tragedy or loss**

Try to find at least one person, more if you can, whom you can talk to about your thoughts of suicide when things aren't too bad. That way if or when those thoughts get more intense and you're in a crisis, you're not starting from square one with them. It will be easier for you to reach out because you have someone who won't freak out. That person can help you get the help you need if you don't have the steam to get it yourself. In a crisis (with or without your support people) you can always call the National Suicide Prevention Lifeline at 1-800-273-8255.

If you're helping someone else who is feeling suicidal, be upfront and ask straightforward questions about whether they have a plan to kill themselves. Let them know that suicidal ideation is treatable and things can get better. Offer to go with them to the hospital or the doctor. Be a compassionate listener who doesn't diminish or downplay their feelings; encourage them by letting them know they're not alone.

. . . .

NOW DO THIS: Choose one small thing to do or stop doing to take care of your mental health. If you can do the small thing, choose a bigger thing and do that next.

YOU ACTUALLY NEED TO KNOW: Learning how to handle a mental health crisis and building your skills to manage mental illness day-to-day can help you keep life on an even keel.

CHAPTER 14

GRIEVING AT TWENTYSOMETHING

Dealing with Death and Other Big Losses

TWENTYSOMETHING TIP: Grieving is exhausting work that often goes unnoticed, especially once the immediate crisis seems to be over. Giving yourself time, and paying attention to what's happening with your grief, will help you heal well.

Loss is part of life. We all know this but most of us don't spend our days dwelling on it. Probably because our experience tells us that dealing with loss is painful, often awkward, and sometimes devastating. We naturally shy away from all those thoughts and feelings. Our past losses, from small disappointments to monumental life-changing grief, have taught us about our own vulnerability. Vulnerable is something many of us don't want to be. Getting comfortable with grief won't take the pain away—at all—but it can help take the fear of it away, or at least help us deal with it in healthier ways. And that can make all the difference for us and for the people around us.

Different Kinds of Grief

Often when we talk about grief and loss it's in reference to the death of someone who is important to us. Losing a parent, sibling, or significant other, grandparent, close friend, or important mentor can rock us to our core. It may force us to redefine much about ourselves and our sense of the world. Even when a relationship was complicated or estranged, the loss still takes time and energy to process and work through. Those kinds of losses can stop us in our tracks.

There are lots of other losses that can be challenging in their own way too: the end of a significant relationship, losing a job, losing a pet, coming to terms with an illness (your own or someone else's). We mourn the loss of a missed opportunity or a dream we must give up. Though quite different from the loss of a loved one through death, the disorienting effect, and the need to process the loss, can still be significant. Even things that at first seem positive, like finishing college or moving to a new city to start a new job, can also involve a sense of loss as we leave people and places we love behind.

TWENTYSOMETHING TALK

I lost someone who was a very good friend for years. We kind of lost touch after high school. He overdosed after being clean for a few years. It surprised me how devastated I was even after not talking to him for so long. I'm still surprised how vividly I can remember him and how much I miss him. —Alex

I have experienced a loss of physical health/mobility due to degenerative disc disease and the multiple surgeries that followed. I am used to the pain, but the loss (I've talked with many peers in my mental health and chronic pain group) is something we don't think anyone fully "gets over." Yes, I have come to terms that I will never be able to teach yoga like I had always wanted, but that loss is still there. I've found help in finding ways to enjoy the things I love in smaller increments. —Jacqui

Sometimes even the exciting parts of life include a grieving we gloss over. For me it was moving away from home. The comforts of the surroundings from childhood and the quiet of a small town were gone. I had to work through that change in life. And while not as dramatic or obvious as a sudden loss, it took introspection. Grief comes in so many ways at so many times. Don't be afraid to name it and work through it. And especially don't ignore it—even when it seems "silly" or "irrational," it's real and deserves attention. —Don

How to Handle It

Identifying the losses you've already experienced and what you learned from them—how did you handle it, what were your biggest struggles, what did you find most helpful at the time, who could you count on—can be helpful preparation for dealing with future losses. Maybe you're in a time of grief right now. How are you doing with that? Have you taken the time to tend to yourself and recognize what the loss means for you? There are different ways to grieve. What helps someone else may not help you. There is no wrong way to do it. Things that are not helpful at one point may be exactly what you need at another time. Here are a few of the ways that people work through a loss:

1. **Spend time alone.** Make sure your schedule has some quiet time each week that you can devote specifically to feeling your feelings and not having to meet other people's expectations.

2. **Create a memorial or project.** When someone dies, pouring the love you have for them into an event or project to remember them—a scholarship fund, a garden, a benefit concert—can help you feel productive and can be a visible way for people to show their support.

3. **Delve into art or music.** Both as an audience member and as a participant in creating, the arts have a healing ability beyond words or thought. Many people dealing with loss find that they can express themselves and find meaning, or simply relief, in making or observing art.

4. **Journal.** Writing down feelings, keeping track of how you're handling life, or just recording memories can all be healing, positive ways to manage grief.

5. **Go to therapy.** Getting connected with a grief counselor or seeing a general therapist while you're grieving can help you learn about the grieving process, understand what is normal, manage any other issues you struggle with, and know that you've got a time set aside to tend to yourself.

6. **Attend a support group.** Being surrounded by others who are also navigating grief can help you feel less isolated. It can also give you a place to express thoughts that can be hard to communicate to some of the folks in your everyday life.

7. **Participate in religious observances and prayer.** Many religious traditions have special days to remember the dead or prayer services for those who are grieving. If

you are religious (and sometimes even if you're not) these can offer a different kind of consolation and support.

8. **Gather a community/have a network of support.** Whether you gather these folks together physically or you just keep a mental list of people you can call on, have at least a small circle of folks you can connect with to help you stay afloat.

9. **Seek out joy and laughter.** When you are exhausted from crying or sick of feeling numb, humor calibrated to your current need can really help. It may be slapstick, stupid, or goofy stuff that helps. Dark comedy or sarcasm may strike you right at some points. Watching silly animal or kid videos, or anything that can make you smile a little, might help.

10. **Read.** Reading to learn more about the grieving process or other people's stories of similar loss can help you feel less isolated and more understood. Reading to escape your current reality and inhabit another world or set of ideas can also be just what you need.

You may find there are times you need company and other times you need solitude. Confusingly there may even be times when you want both at once. Whatever the loss is that you're grieving, and whatever strategies you discover work for you, try to stay tethered to at least a few people who will check up on you, and be sure to give yourself time. Grief keeps its own calendar. You may find you're doing well for a while and then something pulls you back to the center of your grief: a birthday or holiday, a song or a memory. Learning how to manage the strong feelings that come along with grief and keep on living your life at the same time isn't easy. Give yourself the permission to not always get it right.

TWENTYSOMETHING TALK

Everyone grieves each loss differently than the last and differently than others. Listen to advice, but listen to yourself too. Be aware of what triggers the grief, what settles the grief, whatever is going on. Talk to others to process, but don't expect answers from them because only you can understand what's going on. Oh, and as cliché as it sounds, if you're aware and open to working through it, it really does get better with time. —Don

Go to therapy. When I was twenty-three, my dad died, and I broke up with my boyfriend in the same month. I feel I owe so much to my counselor at the time for validating and helping me process all of my very complicated feelings. He even helped me find the perspective to see new beginnings in those big changes, which turned what could have been a very dark time into an opportunity to grow and even thrive. I actually only saw him for six weeks as he was in a temporary position in between my semesters at school, but even that made a huge difference. Thanks, Erik, wherever you are! —Taylor

Reach out to people and don't isolate yourself for long. It's normal and healthy to have time to yourself to process your loss and figure out how you'll get through it. Find community or other support groups. It helps to be around people who have experienced loss. Grief comes in waves. Months may go by after feeling fine and then a memory hits you and you plummet back into your grief. Often unexpectedly. You'll never be fully "recovered" from loss, but you get better at coping with time. —DeAnna

Fill up your calendar with people who support and love you. —Lauren

There are healthy ways and less healthy ways to deal with grief and loss. Withdrawing a bit and giving yourself more time alone is good. Cutting off all contact with the outside world, not so good. Some people throw themselves into a new relationship (or several), which can be a welcome distraction, but the grief doesn't actually go away—it goes on pause and will still need to be dealt with at some point. Some people drink to get a little relief from the pain, but keep an eye on your consumption of alcohol and drugs when you're grieving. It's easier for things to slip out of control when you're dealing with the aftermath of loss. If you start to have difficulty managing your anger or other strong emotions, or you're starting to have suicidal thoughts, talk to your therapist or doctor.

Complicated Grief

When you lose a person, relationship, job, or community that may have both helped and hurt you, it can be a challenge to move through that loss in healthy ways. If you are in a bereavement group or seeing a therapist, they will most likely be well versed in complicated grief. But we don't always have models in our everyday lives of how to grieve the loss of a person who mistreated or abandoned us: a deadbeat dad, an unfaithful ex, someone who was abusive or unkind or unpredictable. When a person like that dies, our chance to confront the mistreatment, the hope for an apology, or some kind of reconciliation or closure dies with them. When we leave a bad relationship or cut off contact with a family member (or our entire family), even though we choose it for our own safety or sanity, it will still hurt some of the time. It is okay to miss the parts that were good even while we remember why we're no longer spending time together. A job that we loved but left because it was destroying us or a community that implodes because of unhealthy leadership or some other calamity is still a significant loss and worthy of our attention.

Funeral Etiquette

It can be strange to suddenly find yourself planning a funeral or trying to figure out an appropriate way to honor someone you've lost. If you are the person responsible for planning a funeral service, there are many guides available. You can often look to funeral home staff or religious leaders to guide you through the steps. Some religious traditions have very formal structures to their funeral service and others have a great deal of flexibility. If there are songs or readings that are not allowed at the service itself, keep in mind those things can be included in other ways—if there is a reception or meal following the service, they can be shared there or in social media posts remembering the person who has died. If you are a support person to someone responsible for planning a funeral, serving as a sounding board for them or helping with the many decisions and details that must be handled in the days surrounding a death can be an incredible gift.

If you are invited to the service, you should make every effort to attend. Even if you are not a religious person and the funeral is centered around the person's faith, attend to show support for the grieving person. Dress appropriately, listen respectfully, participate as invited to do so. It may feel awkward, but the comfort you offer your friend by being there for them cannot be overstated.

When People Say the Wrong Thing

Many people are just bad at dealing with other people's pain. In their own discomfort or nervousness they may say things that are kindly meant but unknowingly hurtful. They might say things that seem thoughtless because they're (unconsciously) trying to shield themselves from the other person's pain. Knowing that this will happen won't keep you from being hurt when it does inevitably occur, but it can lessen the impact a bit. If you are able to hear the intended compassion behind inappropriate comments, that can help. Not everyone is able to do that. And if the wrong person or comment catches you in an exhausted or overwrought moment, it can be very difficult to handle gracefully. Try to think ahead about how you would respond to an insensitive comment or action. A simple, "Thank you for being here," or "Thanks for remembering us," followed by a quick pivot to an innocuous topic can save the day. It can also help if you have someone nearby who can rescue you from these kinds of folks with a quick signal.

Offering Support

How can you care for and support someone you're close to after they've experienced a loss? It's hard to know the right thing to say, and we're often afraid to say the wrong thing. Even if you're not a words person, remember that the best ways to help a grieving person are often by doing the right things rather than saying the right things. And there's so much we can do. A person who is grieving expends much of their usual energy on grief, and everyday tasks can be burdensome. Do their grocery shopping for them or take care of their pet or laundry. Ask if there is something you can help with, but also use your knowledge of them to make specific offers. "Let me know if you need anything," is often too vague an offer for a grieving person to consider or take you up on. Say instead, "I'd like to help. Would it be okay if I do x?" Sometimes the best kind of support you can offer is just being that friend who can sit and listen or keep the bereaved person company and be comfortable with their tears or stories or silence.

Eileen Casey-Campbell, a Unitarian Universalist minister, explained the three rules of hospital chaplaincy:

1. Let the heart have its day. Meaning, let the grieving person feel all their feelings, weep, wail, pound fists, throw things around, stay in bed all day. No "at leasts" or "think of the upside." Not even "it's okay."

2. Postpone long-term decision-making. If you can, help the person grieving delay big life-changing choices like deciding to move, change jobs, start/end relationships, etc.

3. When the ground comes out from under you, dig for bedrock. Ask the questions that lead someone to what their firm foundation is; help them frame the story of their grief in the context of their deepest beliefs. Dig for the prayers, sayings, stories, songs, they've always held on to because those will hold them now.[1]

TWENTYSOMETHING TALK

Resist the urge to give advice. Just validate your friend's feelings. Tell them it's understandable that they feel this way. Listen and let them unload and occasionally repeat things back so they know you're actively listening. —Brandon

I always appreciate it when people don't make it into the misery Olympics. I think it's a natural human attempt at empathy, but when you say, "X bad thing happened to me," and someone responds, "Oh that's terrible! Xish bad thing happened to me, so I know," I find that a bit minimalizing. Letting people feel without comparison is better in my opinion. —Greg

Some other ways to support a grieving friend:

1. **Show up for the service.** If you can't be there, send a card, but make every effort to show up. It matters.
2. **Let them lead.** People need different things at different times. Sometimes they need to talk or just be with you, sometimes they need a distraction. Ask what they need.
3. **Nourish them.** Bring food over. Get them gift cards for takeout. Cook together. Get their groceries.
4. **Remember times that might be hard.** The anniversary of the person's death, birthdays, holidays, religious observances can all be difficult and isolating kinds of days. Reach out or send a note and let them know you are thinking of them, that you remember. Holiday decorating or baking might overwhelm them, so offer to help.
5. **Offer to go with them.** Accompany them to anything that might be difficult: a support group, the lawyer, therapy. It might be awkward for you, but it's definitely harder for them.
6. **Make the calls.** Offer to make phone calls or handle tasks that might be hard right now: cleaning a closet or going through boxes or storage that belonged to the deceased.
7. **Share.** If you knew the person who died, share stories and memories. If you have photographs, share them. If you didn't know the person who passed away, ask

about them. Let your friend know you like to hear their stories.

8. **Get comfortable.** Even if you're not a person who normally hugs or cries, get comfortable with hugs and tears. Let the person know you're here for all of it.

. . . .

NOW DO THIS: Take the time to name what you are grieving—whether it's a person, a relationship, or a situation. Make a list of doable activities or action steps that might help you move toward healing.

YOU ACTUALLY NEED TO KNOW: The big questions of meaning sometimes return with a vengeance, and it can be hard to find normal again. Find a new normal by taking good care of yourself and getting the support you need as you grieve.

PART 5

BECOMING YOURSELF

CHAPTER 15

GETTING A SECOND CHANCE

Forgiveness Is for Grown-Ups (This Means You)

TWENTYSOMETHING TIP: Maybe you screwed up at work or messed up with your housemates. Perhaps you forgot a friend's big event or said the wrong thing to that cutie you've just started dating. Whatever the offense, a good apology can't hurt. Sometimes it can even make things better than before.

The ability to apologize is a life skill that can make everything easier—friendships, romance, family dynamics, work. If you're good at it already, or do it easily, count yourself lucky. Many of us aren't. We didn't learn it growing up and have had to learn the hard way: by doing it badly or not at all. That inability can cost us relationships and opportunities and take a heavy toll on our self-esteem.

Even if we're not terrible at it, many of us don't like having to apologize. It connects us to our weak points. It makes us feel vulnerable. Depending on how it was handled by authority figures earlier on in our lives, it can be associated with shame and embarrassment. No wonder so many people have negative feelings about saying "I'm sorry." But, when we take time to look at the positives, we may find the strength and motivation to get better at seeking forgiveness. It's the right thing to do. It makes us stronger and braver. It can strengthen our relationships. Knowing that we have the skills to repair a mistake or hurt can reduce our anxieties about losing the relationship. Apologizing makes us more accountable to ourselves and to the people we care about.

Some Apology Basics

While every apology is unique and the circumstances are different for each, there are some good general rules to follow:

1. **Be quick to apologize.** While it's tempting to put off apologizing, thinking we might feel more like it later, it often becomes more difficult to do the longer you wait. Waiting to apologize also runs the risks that you'll continue to corrode the relationship. The only time waiting is helpful is if the offended party communicates that they want a delay.

2. **Use your words.** Gestures of apology are great—completing the task you didn't, giving a thoughtful gift—but they are not an actual apology. If you can't bring yourself to speak the words, at least write them down. A note or letter can be a good way to start the conversation, but a conversation still needs to happen.

3. **Never add a "but."** Whether there are other issues to be addressed, if you owe an apology, try to have a conversation that is only about that.

4. **Keep calm.** Losing your temper in the course of apologizing can cause more harm to the relationship than not apologizing at all.

5. **Be well rested and well fed.** Especially if you anticipate high emotions, be as ready as you can be and as "at your best" as possible. It will reduce the chances of saying or doing something wrong because you were crabby, cranky, or overwrought.

6. **Recognize your own patterns.** Is the thing you're apologizing for a rerun? Has this habit been a problem in other relationships? Notice what you get defensive about in the conversation and let that be your teacher. You can get better at these things, really!

7. **Do not assume you'll be forgiven.** Despite a good, heartfelt apology, you may not receive a positive response. Apologizing is still the right thing to do, even if the other person isn't ready to forgive you.

According to Chaplain Paula Kampf, "Forgiveness consists of giving up the desire to make the past better than it was."[1] We need to let go of what we wish had happened and deal with the reality of what actually happened. Like any kind of exercise, when we flex our apology muscles, they get stronger. Be in the habit of apologizing. When you make something a habit, doing it becomes easier (see chapter 12 on habits). Those little everyday acknowledgments of having messed up can help us see that it's not the end of the world to admit we were wrong. It also makes it easier to seek forgiveness when the big important things come along.

How to Construct an Apology

What are the actual words that need to be said? When you construct your apology, try to describe the wrongdoing first. Then say sorry. Here's an example: "I was selfish and inconsiderate, and I really should have asked your opinion before I acted, and I am very sorry for that."

Now you try:

I did/said _____

That (check one):

☐ was wrong
☐ hurt you
☐ made things more difficult for you
☐ other _____

I'm sorry / I apologize

And if appropriate try adding:

Could I do something to make things better?

Revealing that you understand the way in which your action affected the other person and taking responsibility for that action can change everything. It takes humility and courage. At the same time an apology can't be conditional. You apologize to grant the other person the relief of knowing that you understand the impact of your action on them.

TWENTYSOMETHING TALK

Be careful *how* you apologize. The specific words and the intention matter. Don't say, "I'm sorry you feel that way," but rather, "I'm so sorry.

Let's work on this together to get it to a better solution for both of us." It shows that you care about the other person's side of the issue and are willing to resolve it. —Rich

---

At Work

Learning to acknowledge a mistake or habit that has negatively impacted someone else, take responsibility for it, and do what you can to make it right is a vital element of success. With coworkers, supervisors, and customers, apologizing well can build trust and shows maturity. When your failure to do your part has placed an undue burden on someone else at work, be sure to show both your contrition and your appreciation to that person. Be open to what the other person has to say, and rather than defend or respond, listen and let them know that you'll think about what they've said. If it's someone "under" you in the organization, it's no less important. Those are often the people who will make your work life easier (or harder!), and tending those relationships is not only the right thing to do but also can considerably improve your day-to-day happiness at work.

If you owe an apology to a supervisor or someone up the ladder, know that you are probably not the first person who has had to apologize, and you won't be the last. Let that knowledge help you be calm and open when it comes to trying to repair the wrong. Some people at work can receive an apology graciously. Those folks will meet you halfway when it comes to improving things for the future and help you see where you could do better. Others will be terrible at it, and there's little you can do about that except do your best and move on.

Among Friends

In the past you were often surrounded by peers with lots of opportunities to meet new people. And maybe you still are (which is great), but most people's friendship potential goes down tremendously between the ages of eighteen and twenty-three. Given that, the friendships you already have are that much more valuable and usually worth working at. One of the biggest elements of that "work" is reconciliation. Forgiving in friendship can be challenging because it's often easier to let things slide than it is to address them. Letting resentments build can take a long-term toll on a friendship, so try to be in the habit of apologizing for wrongs and checking in to be sure things are okay. If things seem strained or you haven't heard from a friend in a while, check in. Avoid being defensive if your friend does want to talk about something you've done wrong or a habit you have that may hurt them. If you are the wronged party, have the courage to bring up the hard subject. Friends who can forgive each other also help each other grow and become better people.

With Family

Family can be one of the hardest arenas of our lives when it comes to forgiveness. There are often layers of hurt and histories of unfairness, perceived or real, which are wrapped around every story of injury or harm within a family. In many cases a current wrong can stir up all the past wrongs, so what you're dealing with isn't just today's offense but all the offenses that ever happened. For example, if you say something snotty or unkind to a sibling, it may stir up for them every rotten thing you did or said growing up. In your defense, they may have been rotten to you, too, but that's a different discussion. If a family member's reaction to something you've done or said seems out of proportion with today's offense, you may want to take the time (once everyone has calmed down) to address the way your relationship has been in the past and see if repairs are needed there.

With a Significant Other

Reconciliation is the glue that holds a relationship together over the long haul. If saying "I'm sorry" is not something you're good at, get good at it. When vulnerability and intimacy include the ability to make a mistake and be forgiven, when you can admit you were wrong, when you can keep building up the ability in a relationship to give and receive forgiveness, so many other obstacles can be overcome. Without reconciliation, any obstacle can be the one that destroys the relationship.

When You Shouldn't Apologize

Anytime you have the urge to apologize, you probably should. Most of the time you can trust your gut about the need for an apology. There are a few exceptions to that rule. If you're in a relationship in which you find yourself apologizing simply to avoid conflict, you may need to take a closer look at that. It can be a sign that something deeper is wrong. It may be that you've simply established some unhealthy habits, or it could be more serious. When one person lies to manipulate the other or tries to get them to question their own sanity, it's called gaslighting. This is one of several different methods that emotionally abusive people use to control others.

If you're dealing with someone who has a personality disorder or addiction issue, or if you're in a physically or emotionally abusive relationship, no amount of apologizing will be able to fix what's wrong (see chapter 11 for more on dealing with some of those issues). Continuing to apologize when the fault is not yours can have serious consequences for you, including stress, depression, and other mental health and physical symptoms.

Much has been made of women's tendency to over-apologize. Some argue that women should just stop apologizing so much. In an ideal world that would make a lot of sense. And it's certainly worthwhile for women to examine their written and spoken communications and reduce the number of times they apologize unnecessarily, both at work and in personal relationships. At the same time, we live in a fundamentally unequal society where women who fail to follow cultural norms are often judged more harshly. Maintaining relationships and smoothing over conflict in ways that allow tasks to be completed also tends to fall unequally on the shoulders of women.

Georgetown professor of linguistics Deborah Tannen said, "Apologizing is a natural part of our language, and the idea of over-apologizing is subjective."[2] She pointed out that men and women use language, including apologies, differently. "I think the question should be, 'Why do we stigmatize apologies?'"[3] So if you're a woman, be a little bit shrewd about your apologies. Understand that at times it will serve you best to follow the cultural norms and at other times it will pay to buck them. And if you're not a woman, cut your sisters some slack when it comes to how frequently they apologize, and recognize that, much of the time, there's no way for them to win on this one.

Forgiving Yourself

Learning to be kind and forgiving toward other people can be challenging. Learning to be kind and forgiving toward yourself can be the hardest thing of all. Allowing ourselves the same grace that we offer others—being able to make mistakes and have failings—can release us from the heavy weight of self-criticism. When we can't forgive ourselves we tend to carry that baggage around with us. We continue to make ourselves miserable, which inevitably means we're sharing that misery with the people we encounter every day.

Steps Toward Self-Forgiveness

If forgiving yourself is something you struggle with regularly, or if there's the One Big Thing that you can't seem to forgive yourself for, try one of these approaches:

1. **Practice self-compassion.** If this were someone else's mistake or wrongdoing, would you be holding them to

the standard you're holding yourself to? If you can have compassion for another person in this circumstance, maybe you can have it for yourself too.

2. **Talk to someone you trust.** Speak in confidence to someone reliable about your struggle to forgive yourself. Name out loud what you did and how it makes you feel. Some people find that talking about it breaks the spell of awfulness and shame.

3. **Remember that we learn from our mistakes.** Odds are the next time you are in the same situation you'll make a different choice. Let that knowledge help free you from eternally condemning yourself for what you thought was a good choice at the time.

4. **Recognize negative thought patterns.** Often when self-recriminations start playing on repeat in our heads, it's less a sign that we're terrible people and more a symptom that we may be in a bad place emotionally or on the verge of burnout. Learn to self-check when those negative thoughts won't stop, and take steps to take care of yourself with sleep, food, breaks from work or stress, and reaching out to people who care about you.

5. **Get spiritual.** If you come from a religious or spiritual tradition that's been a healing force for you in the past, revisit those teachings and look for the mercy and love there. If that tradition is part of the reason you can't seem to forgive yourself, it may be time to shed that part of your past and get active about adopting a practice that can move you toward wholeness.

If you're finding that this particular thing that you can't forgive yourself for is something that seems to keep happening, take some time to reflect on that. Is there a habit or addiction that is causing or contributing to the problem? Are you connected to people who aren't supporting the choices you know you want to be making? It may be time for a bigger change (revisit chapter 12).

TWENTYSOMETHING TALK

Remember you're not perfect and that you're always growing and learning new things. —Gregory

I am really hard on myself. I will berate myself in my head for a long time. I am not entirely sure if you will ever forgive yourself for certain actions, but using these as life lessons and making sure to learn and improve yourself is best. —Tyler

---

NOW DO THIS: Identify two people you owe an apology to—one easy, one hard. Do the easy one first.

YOU ACTUALLY NEED TO KNOW: Everyone needs to fix a mistake now and then. Not all of us have learned how to do it well, or at all. Adding apologizing to your skill set can smooth out a lot of life's rough edges.

CHAPTER 16

THE POWER OF DIFFERENCE

Why Diversity and Inclusion Matter

TWENTYSOMETHING TIP: People who are comfortable
with difference are happier. Work teams that
are more diverse are also more productive and
come up with better solutions.[1] If you grew up in
a place without much diversity, the learning curve
can be steep, but the effort it takes to get good
at dealing with diversity is worth the reward.

Getting comfortable with people who are different from you is a life skill. Many people manage to mostly get along without it (you probably know some of them) to the detriment of society as a whole. But it's worth getting good at dealing with diversity. Rabbi Yonah Schiller described the skill this way: "Our ability to tolerate others is based on our capacity to empathize with them, understand who they are and what is important to them."[2] People who are willing to push outside the familiar confines of working, learning, and socializing only with those who are most like them benefit in several ways. They live lives that are culturally richer. They learn that the world is more complex and more beautiful than they had imagined. They learn to stop and consider that the way they see and experience the world may be different than the way others see and experience it.

If you can step outside your comfort zone, you may find that you start asking better questions. You may make fewer assumptions about people and instead discover a curiosity about them that you didn't know you possessed. You'll even (eventually) feel more at ease and courageous in a wider range of situations.

If you are a person who cares about human dignity or you're beginning to discover and explore your ability to have a positive influence, building your skills around diversity, equality, and social justice is that much more important. Make sure your real-life actions match the beliefs you profess to hold. It's not an easy thing to do. It takes courage, commitment, and a willingness to risk making mistakes.

What If I Mess Up?

The tough news is that you will mess up. If you get out of your usual "safe" circles and start expanding your world to include people of different races, ethnicities, religions, gender identities, sexual orientations, and backgrounds, you will sooner or later make a mistake. You'll do or say the wrong thing. You'll need to backtrack or check yourself or maybe even apologize. Had you stayed in your safety zone, that never would have happened. The mistake is a sign that you are pushing beyond familiar boundaries. So, as you dust yourself off and feel a little bit of shame or embarrassment about your mistake, do two things. First, let that little tiny taste of struggle help you understand how people who are frequent targets of discrimination feel almost every day. Second, let it be a mark of progress—a learning moment in itself and an inspiration to continue to learn more and do more to make your community, workplace, friend group, or family a safe space for every kind of person.

TWENTYSOMETHING TALK

My experiences abroad, working with refugees, and working with diverse student body populations have made overcoming my fears a lot easier for me. One thing I struggled with is that I was too worried about being biased. But realizing everyone has biases and you are not the only one experiencing this is helpful. I also learned that it is okay to ask questions about others' religion, culture, and experiences. This is how you learn, so do not be afraid to ask, given it is in good faith and your words will not offend the other person. —Tyler

Engage with people with sincere curiosity and truly try to understand them vs. trying to exert or support your point of view. Question your point of view often. —Sofia

I try to educate myself. I do not have all the answers, and I will mess up. When that happens, I learn from the experience and try to find supplemental educational materials to learn how I can be better in the future. —Priya

---

Most of us, if we want to get any better at dealing with diversity, have to do it on purpose. It takes a conscious choice because our world tends to be designed to keep us apart. You've probably heard the term "minority" and seen it used to describe several different groups, based on factors including but not limited to race, ethnicity, color, religion, mental or physical disability, sex, sexual orientation, and gender identity or expression.

In the United States, if you're in a culturally dominant group—groups that are in the majority and/or wield more power than other groups (middle class, Christian, white, or male)— there are many influences and structures at work that continually reinforce that dominance. Those same influences could have you go on believing that the way you and your group experience the world is how everyone else does too. They'd also have you believe that it's the "right" way to experience it. If you're in one of the dominant groups but would rather be part of the solution than part of the problem, here are a few ways to begin taking that on:

1. **Expand your intake.** Push out the boundaries on the kinds of people you come into contact with in the virtual and art world to include voices you may not have heard before. Follow folks on social media from groups you may not encounter every day. Watch the movies and read the books, listen to the music, eat the foods. It can help you start to see that others may be experiencing the world quite differently than you are.

2. **Encounter others.** If you have the chance to join someone from a different faith tradition at their ritual meal or go with them to their place of worship, take it! You don't need to just rely on personal connections though; you can also seek these opportunities out in your community. Many cities (and some rural areas) have interfaith organizations that sponsor events designed to educate and connect. In-person encounters help break down myths and misconceptions in ways that don't happen through reading or research.

3. **Join up.** Find a change-making organization whose mission you can get behind. One of the best ways to learn is to get involved with others who are doing the same.

Interfaith groups, racial justice groups, disability rights organizations, and LGBTQIA+ groups are just some of the groups where you can start doing the real work of diversity and inclusion.

4. **Learn.** Learn about cultural competence (knowledge based) and cultural humility (self-awareness about the limits of our own knowledge).[3] Both are valuable tools in the effort toward dealing with diversity. Read about ways to become an ally.

5. **Use your privilege.** Privilege, in this context, is "a set of unearned benefits given to people who fit into a specific social group."[4] Think about the things you have that you didn't earn—access to certain people or places, family wealth or connections, the benefit of the doubt you get because of your sex, the color of your skin, or your socioeconomic status. You can share some of them with people who have less privilege than you through advocacy, making sure their voices are heard, making introductions, raising issues that will benefit them with people who might not listen to them.

TWENTYSOMETHING TALK

In school and currently where I live, diversity is a challenge because segregation is subconsciously and socioeconomically upheld. It means that even the most well-intentioned of people react and speak in intolerant ways. I have noticed that being the only person of color in my previous friend groups was a manner of status for them; that is, my tokenship provided them with the ability to say that they knew someone like me and could speak to my life experiences as if they were truly knowledgeable. I will get glares and stares as I eat at restaurants because people of my race tend not to live in those areas. In that way, I feel othered and have had to become a person who is self-minded first and foremost. —Marcus

I'm a Latina woman working in a predominantly white male industry: manufacturing consulting. It's generally a challenge, but I haven't figured out how to make a difference. —Sofia

I struggle with the lack of diversity and experience with diversity when I go back home. People there say and do stuff that would be harmful to those who are not like them. I believe that this is due to ignorance and lack of experience. This is always a challenge because when I do speak up, my family has no idea what I am talking about. This can lead to awkward Christmas dinner conversations. —Tyler

I cannot name a specific experience that was a challenge because the lack of diversity in my entire life was a huge challenge. I am a queer brown woman of color who was adopted by a white family. There have been so many instances where others' privileges have caused me problems. I learned how to recognize microaggressions and how to start the process to allow myself to be mad. —Priya

Growing up in a predominantly white community being a woman of color was difficult. I've experienced racism my whole life, but I've realized that I have to take those life experiences and do something with them. I have to advocate for myself and those who don't have a voice so that change happens. —Kay

Twelve Diversity and Inclusion Terms to Know

Catalyst is a global nonprofit that works with business leaders to help build workplaces that are more inclusive and foster success, particularly for women. Here's how the organization describes its list of terms to know: "This list isn't exhaustive, nor is it the final word. As the D&I field develops, many of these terms may evolve too. The point: We all keep learning, and growing our vocabulary, together."[5]

Ally

Noun: Advocates for people from underrepresented or marginalized groups. An ally takes action to support people outside of their own group.

Cisgender

Adj: A term used to describe people whose gender identity matches the sex they were assigned at birth. Often abbreviated to cis.

Corporate Social Responsibility

Noun: Practicing good corporate citizenship by going beyond profit maximization to make a positive impact on communities and societies.

Emotional Tax

Noun: The combination of being on guard to protect against bias, feeling different at work because of gender, race, and/or ethnicity, and the associated effects on health, well-being, and ability to thrive at work.

Equality

Noun: Treating everyone the same way, often while assuming that everyone also starts out on equal footing or with the same opportunities.

Equity

Noun: Working toward fair outcomes for people or groups by treating them in ways that address their unique advantages or barriers.

Intersectionality

Noun: The intertwining of social identities such as gender, race, ethnicity, social class, religion, sexual orientation, and/or gender identity, which can result in unique experiences, opportunities, and barriers.

Neurodiversity

Noun: The concept that there is great diversity in how people's brains are wired and work, and that neurological differences should be valued in the same way we value any other human variation.

Non-Binary (also known as *Genderqueer*)

Adj: A category for a fluid constellation of gender identities beyond the woman/man gender binary.

Unconscious Bias

Noun: An implicit association, whether about

people, places, or situations, which [is] often based on mistaken, inaccurate, or incomplete information and [includes] the personal histories we bring to the situation.

Work-Life Effectiveness

Noun: A talent management strategy that focuses on doing the best work at the best time with the best talent. It helps businesses create flexibility, enhance agility, and drive mutually beneficial solutions for both employers and employees.

Workplace Inclusion

Noun: An atmosphere where all employees belong, contribute, and can thrive. Requires deliberate and intentional action.[6]

TWENTYSOMETHING TALK

We live in a globalized world that's only getting more interconnected, and being aware and respectful of differences is becoming more and more of a minimum requirement to navigate our world. Plus, a lot of fear and prejudice is based on a lack of understanding or exposure, so exposing yourself to diverse communities and individuals can make society all-around better. Get to know people from different backgrounds, and if that's not necessarily possible, there's always the option of reading books from authors representing different backgrounds to see the world/life from different perspectives. —Bridget

NOW DO THIS: First choose a lower-risk activity to increase your diversity awareness. You could read a book by an author from a different background or follow some thought leaders on social media who have a different perspective. Next choose a higher-risk activity. You could attend an event or get involved in a project.

YOU ACTUALLY NEED TO KNOW: Dealing with difference takes courage, practice, and a bit of selflessness. The world opens up in some really wonderful ways as you get better at dealing with, and then appreciating, diversity.

CHAPTER 17

MAKING YOUR LIFE MATTER

TWENTYSOMETHING TIP: Some people know what they are "meant" to do from early on. For others, it takes some trial and error. It's okay to not know. It's also okay to make a course correction, change your mind, or recognize that the reasons you were on a certain path have changed.

"Let your life speak." The writer Parker Palmer tells of discovering this old Quaker saying as a young man. Initially, he thought it was about living up to the demanding standards of the highest truths he could find. Over time, and after spending a great deal of energy doing what he thought he was "supposed to do," he came to a very different conclusion about those words. His revised understanding is gentler, truer, and wiser. He came to understand "let your life speak" to mean:

> Before you tell your life what you intend to do with it, listen for what it intends to do with you. Before you tell your life what truths and values you have decided to live up to, let your life tell you what truths you embody, what values you represent.[1]

Dr. Christine Whelan is a clinical professor in the School of Human Ecology at the University of Wisconsin-Madison. Her approach is for people to understand the "what" and the "why" of their lives in a holistic way—to have a purpose mindset. What does that mean? Dr. Whelan wrote, "Living purposefully means having a good sense of what you are trying to accomplish in your life—and an understanding of why it's important."[2]

Using those two different but overlapping approaches—first,

let your life speak and second, have a purpose mindset—let's take a look at where you are right now and where you'd like to be. What *does* your life tell you? To answer that question, consider questions such as: What do you love? What are you good at? What don't you mind working hard to get good at? If someone who didn't know you looked at your life from the outside—how you've spent your time so far, what you've done for work and fun, who you spend your time with, what you talk about, read about, care about—what values might they say you represent? And what *are* you trying to accomplish in your life? What matters to you and why does it matter? To answer those questions, think about some of these questions: What are your core values? What do you believe? What do you have energy for? What conclusions have you come to about the world and your place in it? What conclusions have you come to about yourself?

What Do You Do?

Maybe your job right now is meaningful and gives you the opportunity to live out your values. If you're lucky, the work you do to make your living leaves you feeling like you have a life. If you're really lucky it also pays you enough to live on. You've hit the career jackpot if you've got all that and at least some of your coworkers are people you like, respect, or admire. Does that all sound like a fairytale? For a lot of people, their job is simply a way to pay the bills and the "living out values" and "making meaning" parts come from what they do with their time outside of work.

Depending on what's happening at this moment in your life, it might be hard to even think about questions of meaning. Maybe you're not working right now or not settled in your work. Maybe you're at a deciding place: choosing between work or more school or some other big life choice. If you have an illness or disability that keeps you from having what a lot of people think of as regular work, making meaning can be a different kind of struggle. Chronic pain, health challenges, and limited energy can be at odds with the desire to create, to accomplish, and sometimes even just to be.

So this conversation isn't just about your job. It's about what your dreams are. It's about your relationships, your obligations, your commitments, and your passions and creating a life that you love living. It's also about discovering what has meaning for you now, regardless of what you might have wanted to be or to accomplish in the past. Those things can and do change with time and experience.

TWENTYSOMETHING TALK

My sense of purpose comes from my self-image, the roles I assign myself, and my aspirations. My religious/spiritual life and relationships are also a factor. My self-image is a big one though; I have goals I want for myself in terms of my character and position in life and who I want to be. That is my strongest force. —Marisa

My mom is my rock. This has changed over the course of my life, however the base seems to always be family. Volunteering has also been very high in my life at times. But typically, when boiling everything down, it comes to family. —Kay

Are You Happy?

Happiness is tricky. Most of us know at least one person who has mistaken pleasure for happiness (or at least tried to substitute it), which can lead to all sorts of problems. But happiness, real happiness, occurs when what we're doing matches up with what we believe and value.

Here are a few approaches that might move you closer to it:

1. Take time to discover the people, places, causes, and communities that help you experience a sense of joy and purpose in your life. If you're not sure how to do that, start by revisiting chapter 10. Find ways to volunteer, make a difference, and make meaning.

2. Work on becoming the person—friend, partner, sibling, offspring, worker, artist—you want to be using personal goal setting. This includes doing your inner work as an adult: recovering from the hurts of your past, going deep in your relationships, building the skills you need to develop relationships that are rich with meaning and connection.

3. Compare the values you hold now to those you followed

during your upbringing. Are your values and beliefs pretty similar or dramatically different? Maybe somewhere in the middle. In chapter 9 we discussed some of the less-than-healthy ways that families can exercise power and control. Take the time to decide what values you want to hang on to or let go of and what new ones you'd like to adopt.

4. Find your spiritual teachers and identify your adult system of values and spirituality. Grow up your religious life in the same ways you are growing up your work and social life. Revisit chapter 15 for more on this.

5. Make a life instead of making a living. No one wishes on their death bed that they'd spent more time at the office. But when you have work that is meaningful and matches up with your values, it's perfectly fine to pursue it vigorously.

Mike Hayes, director of young adult ministry in the Diocese of Cleveland and author of *Loving Work*, asks, "If you could do *anything*, how would you want to spend your time? What's the most important way you could spend time?"[3] It's worth taking the time to figure out your answer (or answers) to that question.

TWENTYSOMETHING TALK

These are some things I've learned recently and am reminding myself when I'm feeling overwhelmed or anxious: Comparing yourself to others does nothing; it accomplishes nothing. Everyone is on their own path.

What you're doing right now doesn't define who you are or where you're going in life, so don't get discouraged. This adulting stuff is *hard*, and comparing your job/grades/relationships to other people will do nothing but create more stress and anxiety. We all have enough of that already. —Marcus

You can have more than one dream/goal. How you get there is as important as achieving it. And changing your goal is okay on the journey. —Chris

Finding who you are is a fun process of exploring what makes your heart explode with joy in your twenties. But don't forget where you came from and what formed you to who you currently are. —Kim

---

NOW DO THIS: Create a small goal around one idea from this chapter that brings you a step closer to loving your life now. Write it here but also post it someplace you'll see frequently, as a reminder on your phone or next to your bed. Once you've accomplished it, check it off and take the next step.

YOU ACTUALLY NEED TO KNOW: Some folks have a big strong sense of mission about their lives, and others are simply seeking happiness. Wherever you fall on that spectrum, a little bit of introspection and some well-focused intention can go a long way toward living a more satisfying life.

FIND YOURSELF A . . .

In a new city you need a whole new set of people, places, and things to help you get your life in order. Keep track here as you find great shops, restaurants, parks, doctors. Write down websites, addresses, and contact info and come back to the list to keep making your new city your own.

☐ Airport:

☐ Bakery:

☐ Bank:

☐ Bookstore:

☐ Bus stop/subway/train station:

☐ Church/mosque/synagogue/temple/gurdwara:

☐ Coffee shop:

☐ Consignment/thrift store:

☐ Dentist:

☐ DMV/government office:

☐ Doctor:

☐ Emergency shelter (earthquake, tornado):

☐ Farmers' market:

☐ Game store:

☐ Grocery:

☐ Gym/yoga studio/martial arts studio/dance studio:

☐ Hairdresser/barber:

☐ Hiking/bike trail:

☐ Hospital/urgent care:

☐ Ice-cream place:

☐ Laundromat:

☐ Library:

☐ Mall/shopping center:

☐ Mechanic:

☐ Music venue:

☐ Park:

☐ Pet shop/pet supply store:

☐ Pharmacy:

☐ Pizza joint:

☐ Place to swim/boat:

☐ Polling place:

☐ Post office:

☐ Restaurant—cheap but good:

☐ Restaurant—fancy:

☐ Specialty food market/restaurant (gluten-free, vegetarian/

vegan, ethnic, etc.):

☐ Stadium:

☐ Twenty-four-hour diner:

☐ Vet:

RENTER'S GLOSSARY

All bills paid: utilities included

Amenities: extra, attractive features that make an apartment building or complex more enjoyable for its tenants (gym, pool, etc.) for which renters may be charged an amenities fee

Apartment: a suite of rooms forming one residence, typically in a building containing a number of these, often owned by a landlord and rented to tenants

Application: a form used by landlords and property management companies to screen potential tenants; there is often a nonrefundable fee charged to process an application

Arrears: either delayed billing (e.g., if water billing cycles are two months in arrears, when you pay your water bill with your March rent, you are paying for water you used in January and February) or the amount by which a particular account is past due

BR/BA: abbreviations for "bedroom" and "bathroom;" e.g., a 2BR/1.5BA place would have two bedrooms, one full bath, and one half bath

Broker/leasing agent: a person who works with a property owner to find tenants for their buildings

Commission: a fee paid by a landlord to a broker/leasing agent in exchange for finding suitable tenants

Common areas: any area of the building outside of your individual apartment, including hallways, laundry rooms, amenity spaces

Concession/incentive/move-in special: anything that encourages prospective tenants to rent a property (e.g., no application fee)

Cosigner/guarantor: a person who is not a tenant but legally agrees to pay rent to the landlord in the event that the tenant cannot do so

Cotenants: people who live in and rent a property together, both/all of whom sign the lease and share responsibility for meeting the terms of the lease

Deposit: an amount of money given to a landlord or leasing agent by a prospective tenant ahead of moving in to hold the apartment (may or may not also be used as the security deposit)

Duplex: can be either an apartment with two floors or levels (not two apartment units) or a building with two separate apartment spaces, typically side by side rather than upper/lower

Fair housing / equal opportunity (EOH) laws: laws that protect against discrimination on the basis of race, color, national origin, religion, sex, familial status, and disability for prospective tenants

Full bath: a bathroom containing a tub and/or shower as well as a sink and toilet

Garden-style apartment: low-rise apartment community; one to three floors, may or may not have elevators, sometimes surrounded by lawn or greenspace (not condos, townhomes, or luxury apartments).

Gentrification: the process of repairing and rebuilding homes and businesses in a deteriorating area (such as an urban neighborhood) accompanied by an influx of middle-class or affluent people, which often results in the displacement of earlier, usually poorer residents

Guest: a person who visits a tenant, and may sleep over occasionally, but is not listed on the lease and is not responsible for paying rent or meeting the terms of the lease

Habitable: meeting basic living condition requirements (has heat and running water, is free from health and safety hazards)

Half bath: a bathroom with a sink and toilet but no tub or shower

Kitchenette: a small kitchen or area of a larger room used for food preparation and storage but possibly lacking full-sized appliances; found in studio/bachelor/efficiency apartments

Landlord: the owner of a rental property

Lease: a legal contract stating an agreement between a landlord and tenant, including the terms and conditions expected for a rental property, usually for a period of twelve months

Lease takeover/lease assignment: when a new tenant takes over the remaining term of a departing tenant's lease, with the approval of the landlord (unlike a sublease, the original tenant is no longer responsible for meeting the terms of the lease)[1]

Lessee: a tenant who has agreed to a lease

Lessor: a landlord who has agreed to a lease

Loft: a large, open space, usually without any internal walls (except for the bathroom), often in a formerly industrial building that has been converted into residential apartments

Mixed use: an area or building that combines commercial and residential properties

Month-to-month/monthly: a rental that offers leases with a term no longer than one month

Normal wear and tear: a reasonable amount of wear an apartment is expected to experience within a lease term

Notice to vacate: prior notification from the tenant to the landlord stating the tenant's intention to leave the rental property (usually a minimum of thirty or sixty days)

Property manager: person who manages a piece of real estate for the owner, including maintaining the property and collecting rent from the tenants

Prorated: proportionately distributed rental fee reflecting less than the full month

Reno/update: a recently updated or renovated apartment unit

Rent control: a government program that places a limit on the amount a landlord can demand for leasing a home or renewing a lease

Rent to own: a lease agreement that provides the tenant with an option to purchase the property

Rental history: rental background (similar to a credit check)

Residential: a property or area designated for people to live; not commercial/business

Security deposit: a payment that a tenant makes to the landlord in the event that there is damage to the property

Studio/efficiency/bachelor apartment: an apartment that lacks a defined bedroom but does include a bathroom and either a full kitchen or kitchenette

Sublet/sublease: when a resident who has leased the premises from the owner rents out that property to another person; the original resident (lessee) is still responsible for paying the rent to the owner (landlord/lessor) through the term of the original lease

Subsidized/Section 8/HUD: housing for low-income families that is paid for in part or in total by the government

Super: short for *superintendent* or *building supervisor*, this is a manager responsible for repair and maintenance in a residential building

Tenant: a person who rents a property

Term: the length of time a landlord and tenant agree to rent

Townhouses/townhomes: a row of houses, often two stories, joined together by sidewalls

Utilities: electricity, gas, water

Walk-through: when the tenant and the landlord or property manager examine the apartment together, either before move-in or after move-out, to note and mark the current condition of the rental

Walk-up: a building of usually three to four stories with no elevator

W/D: washer/dryer; "W/D connection" means that space and proper electrical and plumbing hookups exist for a washer and dryer, but the actual appliances are not included

WIC: Walk-in closet

ACKNOWLEDGMENTS

Many thanks to Joelle Delbourgo, agent extraordinaire, for her early support, wise counsel, steadiness, and dedication to her work. I don't know anyone who is as good at their job as you are.

Right from the start Webster Younce (then of Thomas Nelson, now of Zondervan) understood, valued, and furthered what I wanted to accomplish with this book. Thank you, Webb!

I'm grateful to Brigitta Nortker at Nelson Books who called dibs on the project and whose smart and relevant editing made everything better. Thanks to the rest of the Nelson team too—Emily Ghattas, Rachel Tockstein, Sara Broun, and Shea Nolan—so good!

Dr. Christine Whelan's excellent research and thoughtful responses to my questions about living your purpose helped immensely, thank you.

Thanks to Leora Tanenbaum and the folks at Catalyst.org for allowing me to include part of their article in chapter 16, "12 Diversity and Inclusion Terms You Need to Know."

ACKNOWLEDGMENTS

I appreciate every ministry colleague who helped my thinking, either through your own writing or in conversation or both: Mike Hayes, Becky Eldredge, Paula Kampf, Sarah Jarzembowski, Kim Potter Winden, Fr. Ted Brown, Fr. Larry Rice—to name a few.

I am super thankful to all the twentysomethings who have opened their lives and hearts to me. It was your willingness to be vulnerable, your questions, your searching and seeking that launched this idea in the first place. Specifically, thanks to Lauren Tatanus, who shared her journals and helped me think about the struggles young adults go through in ways I hadn't before. Big thanks to Emily Brennan-Moran for always having the right words just when I needed them, for beautiful insights for the introduction to this book, and for great practical information on how to live in a hot place. I'm grateful to Sarah LoPresti and Al and Kelly Jutsum for looking at early outlines and chapter descriptions and helping me fill the empty spots.

To my survey respondents—your insights and generous sharing moved me. Your comments make this book authentic and true in ways that wouldn't have been possible without you.

I'm grateful to my incredible social media circle who answered so many questions (and questioned a few answers), to every single one of you: THANK YOU!

For those who signed up for even more social media Q&A fun in my book group: Oh my goodness, I love you people! Thank you to: Amanda Grace, Andrea Costello, Ania Beata Owczarczyk, Anne Kidera Gallagher, Brian Anglin, Brian Singer-Towns, Brigit Hurley, Chris Coniglio, Chris Offermann, Christine

Carnahan, Christine Hood, Christine Whitbourne, Colleen King, Courtney Chester, Courtney Forrester, Damita Peace, DeAnna Darling, Denise Mack, Don Smith, Dorie Jennings, Eileen Bradbury Legler, Eric Heveron-Smith, Evan Wilson, Gail Dowd, George Hochbrueckner, Heather Anne Adams Johnson, Helga Shaver Lübbers, Jackie Shiers Leszyk, Jacqui Dümmer, Jean Scoppa Waldmiller, Jennifer Troiano Batz, Jesse Thomas, Joanne Layton, Judi Dutcher, Julie Butson Mickler, Karen Bradbury, Sr. Karen Dietz, Karen Ludwig, Kari Aldridge, Keisha Stokes, Kelley Kelly, Kelly Rife Ide, Kristen Leschhorn, Kristin Forrester Kuhmann, Laure Barr, Lauren Tatanus, Lorrie Boyce, M. Maureen Hood, Mame Maloney, Mary Haas, Mary Kay Williams, Matt Cleary, Monica Bradbury-Lareau, Morgan Chester, Patrick Fox, Robyn Humphrey, Sara Cegelski, Sarah Legler, Sarah LoPresti, Sarah O'Connor, Sr. Laurie Orman, Kim Potter Winden, Skye Smith, Stephanie Lauffer Sonner, and Vicky Wejko.

Forever thanks to my sisters for believing in me—especially Monica Bradbury-Lareau who I could call or message anytime of the day (or more often night) whenever I was stuck and she would unstick me, can tame my feral commas, and who has gone far beyond the call of sisterhood with research and writing (especially chapters 3 and 8).

Thanks to my own young adult offspring: Jonathan, Catherine, Gregory, and Monica for being my first audience, primary brainstormers, reality checkers, and encouragers.

And to Greg Haehl for everything, always.

NOTES

Chapter 2: Fantastic Jobs and Where to Find Them

1. Patricia Reaney, "Dream Job? Most U.S. Workers Want to Change Careers—Poll," Reuters, July 1, 2013, https://www .reuters.com/article/us-usa-work/dream-job-most-u-s-workers -want-to-change-careers-poll-idUSBRE96015Z20130701.
2. LinkedIn Corporate Communications, "New LinkedIn Research Shows 75 Percent of 25–33 Year Olds Have Experienced Quarter-Life Crises," LinkedIn Pressroom, November 15, 2017, https://news.linkedin.com/2017/11/new -linkedin-research-shows-75-percent-of-25-33-year-olds-have-e.
3. Samantha McLaren, "6 Gen Z Traits You Need to Know to Attract, Hire, and Retain Them," *LinkedIn Talent Blog*, October 8, 2019, https://business.linkedin.com/talent-solutions /blog/hiring-generation-z/2019/how-to-hire-and-retain -generation-z.
4. Christine B. Whelan, email message to author, April 30, 2020.

Chapter 3: My Place

1. Paula Pant and Marguerita Cheng, "How to Budget for Your First Apartment," *The Balance*, April 4, 2020, https://www .thebalance.com/how-to-budget-for-your-first-apartment -4113283.

2. Rent Editorial Team, "How to Break a Lease on Your Apartment," Rent.com, February 26, 2019, https://www.rent .com/blog/how-to-break-a-lease/.

Chapter 4: Adulting at Your Parents' House

1. "The Majority of 18–24-Year-Olds Live in Their Parents' Home, as Do 1 in 6 Older Millennials," Marketing Charts, December 4, 2017, https://www.marketingcharts.com /demographics-and-audiences-81471.
2. Kylie Rymanowicz, "Positive Family Communication Starts Early," Michigan State University Extension, August 2, 2017, https://www.canr.msu.edu/news/positive_family _communication_starts_early_part_1.

Chapter 5: Shared Spaces vs. Solitary Places

1. Harlan Cohen, "Getting Comfortable with the Uncomfortable," TEDx at Ursuline College, November 17, 2014, https://www .youtube.com/watch?v=EyY6QR8Geys.
2. Sharon Jayson, "Millennials, Generation Z: Connected with Thousands of Friends—But Feeling All Alone," USA Today, March 7, 2019, https://www.usatoday.com /story/news/health/2019/03/07/millennial-generation-z -social-media-connected-loneliness-cigna-health-study /3090013002/.

Chapter 6: Mmmmm, Delish!

1. "Four Steps to Food Safety: Clean, Separate, Cook, Chill," Centers for Disease Control and Prevention, last reviewed March 18, 2020, https://www.cdc.gov/foodsafety/keep-food -safe.html.

Chapter 7: My Stuff, My Self

1. Cory Stieg, "How You Think about Money Can Impact How Happy You Are in Life, Study Says," CNBC Make It,

September 5, 2019, https://www.cnbc.com/2019/09/05/can
-money-buy-happiness-debate-study-on-success.html.

2. Dinsa Sachan, "Scientific Proof That Buying Things Can Actually Lead to Happiness (Sometimes)," *Fast Company*, July 6, 2016, https://www.fastcompany.com/3061516/scientific-proof -that-buying-things-can-actually-buy-happiness-sometimes.

Chapter 9: Not a Kid Anymore

1. Jeffrey Jensen Arnett, *Emerging Adulthood: The Winding Road from the Late Teens through the Twenties*, 2nd ed. (New York: Oxford University Press, 2015), 9.

2. Amanda Barroso, Kim Parker, and Richard Fry, "Majority of Americans Say Parents Are Doing Too Much for Their Young Adult Children," Pew Research Center, October 23, 2019, https://www.pewsocialtrends.org/2019/10/23/majority-of -americans-say-parents-are-doing-too-much-for-their-young -adult-children/.

3. Barroso, Parker, and Fry.

Chapter 10: Fast Friends

1. Ellie Polack, "New Cigna Study Reveals Loneliness at Epidemic Levels in America," Cigna, May 1, 2018, https:// www.multivu.com/players/English/8294451-cigna-us -loneliness-survey/.

2. Renee Stepler, "Number of U.S. Adults Cohabiting with a Partner Continues to Rise Especially Among Those 50 and Older," Pew Research Center, April 6, 2017, https://www .pewresearch.org/fact-tank/2017/04/06/number-of-u-s-adults -cohabiting-with-a-partner-continues-to-rise-especially-among -those-50-and-older/.

Chapter 11: You're Amazing!

1. Meera Jagannathan, "More People Meet Online Than through Friends or Family or Work," MarketWatch, February 12, 2019,

https://www.marketwatch.com/story/more-people-meet-online
-than-through-friends-or-family-or-work-2019-02-12.

Chapter 12: The Good News About Your Bad Habits

1. Sam Kemmis-Zapier, "Procrastination Is an Emotional
   Problem," *Fast Company*, May 31, 2019, https://www
   .fastcompany.com/90357248/procrastination-is-an-emotional
   -problem.
2. "Addiction," *Psychology Today*, https://www.psychologytoday
   .com/us/basics/addiction.
3. Yvonne H. C. Yau and Marc N. Potenza, "Gambling Disorder
   and Other Behavioral Addictions: Recognition and Treatment,"
   Harvard Review of Psychiatry 23, no. 2 (March–April 2015):
   https://www.ncbi.nlm.nih.gov/pmc/articles/PMC4458066/.

Chapter 13: How's Your Brain Doing?

1. "Understanding Mental Health," FindTreatment.gov, Substance
   Abuse and Mental Health Services Administration, October
   2019, https://findtreatment.gov/content/understanding-mental
   -health/know-the-warning-signs/.
2. "Mental Health Conditions," National Alliance on Mental
   Health, https://www.nami.org/Learn-More/Mental-Health
   -Conditions.
3. Susan Biali Haas, "Could 'Relative' Hypoglycemia Be Causing
   Your Anxiety?," *Psychology Today*, October 10, 2018, https://
   www.psychologytoday.com/us/blog/prescriptions-life/201810
   /could-relative-hypoglycemia-be-causing-your-anxiety.
4. Kendra Cherry, "How Social Support Contributes to
   Psychological Health," Verywell Mind, updated April 14, 2020,
   https://www.verywellmind.com/social-support-for-psychological
   -health-4119970.
5. Quentin Fottrell, "Suicide Rate among Young Americans Soars
   by More than 50% over 10 Years," MarketWatch, October 28,
   2019, https://www.marketwatch.com/story/suicide-rate-among